An Alternative History of Mankind

by

John J. Ventre

Cover Art by

Ralph Damiani

LANG PUBLICATION

www.LangPublication.com

All characters appearing in this book are fictional. All political events depicted or referenced in this book are fictitious. Any resemblance to actual political situations, and or real persons, living or dead, is purely coincidental. Statements and opinions expressed in this book are not in any way representative of Lang Publication (the publisher).

Fair Use Notice: This book may contain copyrighted material the use of which has not always been specifically authorized by the copyright owner. I am making such material available in an effort to advance understanding of political, human rights, economic, democracy, scientific, and social justice issues, etc. I believe this constitutes a 'fair use' of any such copyrighted material as provided for in section 107 of the US Copyright Law. In accordance with Title 17 U.S.C. Section 107, the material on this site is distributed without profit to those who have expressed a prior interest in receiving the included information for research and educational purposes. For more information go to: http://www.law.cornell.edu/uscode/17/107.shtml.

If you wish to use copyrighted material from this book for purposes of your own that go beyond 'fair use', you must obtain permission from the copyright owner. Any material in this book can be used for education in the field of Ufology by referencing this book title and author.

Publication Date: March 17, 2014, 2nd printing March 17, 2020.
ISBN: 978-0-9883606-4-8
LANG PUBLICATION
Printed in USA

Word count: 42,706.

TABLE OF CONTENTS

PROLOGUE

"Who's your Daddy?" 5

CHAPTERS

1. Genesis 11
2. Disclosure 81
3. The Case for UFOs 147
4. Trans-Humanism 171
5. Revelation 183
6. Origin of the Phenomena 197
7. About the Author 205
8. References 209

Also by John Ventre

Books:

1625 Project

Case for UFOs

Apophis 2029

The Ufologist

Day After 2012

Wuhan Conspiracy

12/21/2012 A Prophecy

UFOs over Pennsylvania

String Theory of the Unexplained

An Alternative History of Mankind

TV:

Hangar 1

UFO Hunters

Alien Mysteries

UFOs over Earth

Close Encounters

UFOs over Pittsburgh

Anderson Cooper Show

String Theory of the Unexplained

UFO Conspiracy: Hunt for the Truth

Movies:

Kecksburg

Flatwoods

The Exorcism Prayer

Prologue

"Who's your Daddy?"

"The day science begins to study non-physical phenomena; it will make more progress in one decade than in all the previous centuries of its existence." — Nikola Tesla

I WRITE THIS BOOK IN DEFIANCE OF THE AIR FORCE, CIA AND SCIENTIFIC COMMUNITIES!

If you were hoping to read just another run of the mill UFO book, then this book isn't for you. This book will cause you to question everything you've ever been told from science to religion to evolution to Creation. Do not sit up at night and read this story to your Grandchildren for it is a tale of deception much like your life!

Scientists and professors would like you to believe that history, like evolution, moves in a straight line. Scientists want repeatable, verifiable results, but sometimes a phenomenon happens rarely. Anthropologists and Paleontologists love to run the clock backwards using carbon dating, DNA and fossil records. But in fact, the clock is moving forward with genetic modifications, stem cell research and biocompatible computer chips. Will we create a hybrid human race that cannot enter the Kingdom of God or destroy ourselves?

Nearly 100 years since the "Scopes Monkey Trial", evolution teaches that life can't arise and be sustained from a single Adam and Eve. There had to be thousands of first humans for the necessary genetic diversity. The Bible teaches that Adam and Eve's DNA was pure and that mutations have caused our illnesses and shortened life span. Dinosaur fossils are the result of Noah's flood and that evolution is an atheist myth. Yet without Adams original sin, there would be no need for Jesus to come to earth. Science changes but does the word of God? If science cannot prove the theory of evolution, then there is no life in space. The bible is the only book in the world that reads you as you read it! These scientists, as well as religious leaders, will fight to protect their theories. In the course of doing this, they reject, insult, deceive and attempt to debunk evidence conflicting with their ideas. If scientific theory is correct and life arose from lightening striking a primordial soup of chemicals, then why can't science reproduce this chemical reaction? A watch proves a watch maker and life proves God who is the only creator of life!

There has never been a satisfactory explanation for the sudden development of civilization around 4000 BC and the increase in our brain capacity. At that time, mankind experienced the sudden advancement of Samaria, Egypt, Mexico and Peru. According to Evolutionary Biologists, human beings are the result of snail-paced evolution. Then why can we find no archeological evidence of a natural progression? Where are the creatures that are half way morphed into another and why did Cro-Magnon man exist after Homo-sapiens? Instead, we find only missing links and archeology lacking in support of their theories!

There is a global conspiracy of atheistic disinformation, fraud, confirmation bias, cognitive dissonance and consensus science along with a rise in occultism. UFOs are like an iceberg where the sighting is the tip of the iceberg and the submerged portion question archeology, politics, psychology, anthropology, evolution, technology and religion. Our world leaders, led by the

United States, keep the truth from the public, assuming, whether rightly or wrongly, that the people "can't handle the truth." There have been five great extinctions and yet evolution supposedly started all over each time.

Even the Freedom of Information Act regards the public as the "public enemy" when they black out sentences and paragraphs for security reasons. The acceptance of the "Supernatural" or an alternative history would destroy the basis of science taught in our Universities. Therefore, scientists sit in the cheap seats and decide not to play while religious leaders have covertly gotten in the game. But how do you measure a dream?

Through the use of radiometric dating, for example, it has been discovered that the earth periodically cleanses itself and somehow replaces the dominant species with another. This technology has shown many artifacts from all over the world as existing in a time "out of place" and no object that can be radiocarbon dated can be more than 250,000 years old. Then why have dinosaurs been radiocarbon dated with soft tissue still attached to them? Did they die in the Great Flood and that truth would destroy the theory of evolution? Why is there carbon 14 in diamonds and coal deposits when carbon 14 dissipates within 90K years? Why did the Smithsonian Museum cover up the Kincaid Egyptian find in 1909 in Arizona and also remove from their museum the 1500 year old gold airplane trinkets found in Central America when they were discovered to be aerodynamic? Does the

Mount St Helens explosion and flooding demonstrate that disasters produce quick results and quick replenishing as the Bible describes? Radiometric dating of Mount St Helens ten years after the explosion concluded that it occurred millions of years ago. Carbon dating measures the amount of carbon in a static environment. It does not measure the amount of time. There are more evolutionary scientists than proof for evolution which can all be placed on a small table in your kitchen. The epitome of *Fake News* is sciences refusal to put Darwin's theories to the scientific method.

In the film "Planet of the Apes", the Simian leaders would do anything to suppress the truth. As we do today with people, the ape's leaders followed the convenient premise that the apes "can't handle the truth." Like a recessive gene, what truth could be so horrible that our world leaders must protect humanity from its discovery out of fear that this truth could bring down the fabric of our society? Why do humans find their own existence a problem that needs to be resolved? Why can't we look through the cosmic pane of glass that separates us from the truth? Why do we have collective amnesia regarding our ignored history; a history of alien intervention and genetic engineering or God's creation?

When dealing with the UFO question, one must remember:

"And you were dead in your trespasses and sins, in which you formerly walked according to the course of this world,

according to the prince of the power of the AIR (UFOs), of the spirit that is now working in the sons of disobedience." (Ephesians 2:1–2) . . . **also known as the Morningstar and can appear as an angel of light (Orbs)!**

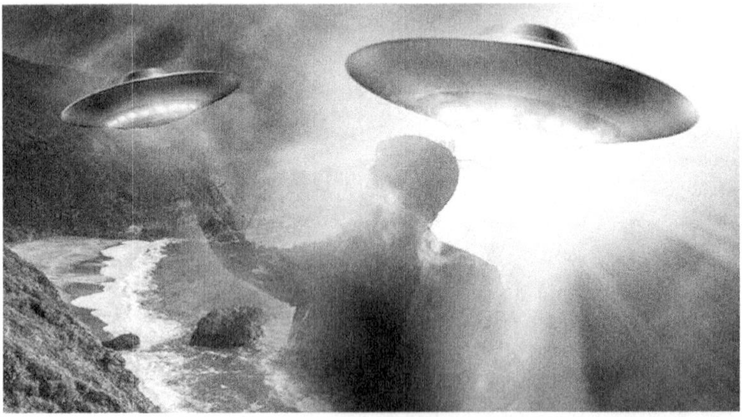

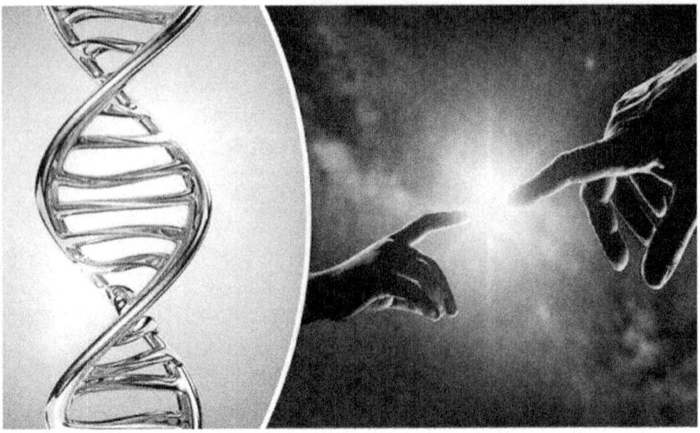

(Courtesy Getty images)

If you read beyond this point, you may lose the protection of God.

Chapter One

Genesis

"If you had to choose which theory is not most provable but which theory is most likely with the least number of missing links, which would you choose in regards to how mankind got here? Is it Creation, Evolution or Intelligent Design meaning alien genetic engineering?" - - - "Putting God aside, genetic engineering has the least flaws and is most likely the strongest theory to explain the origin of us but how do you ignore God?" - - - John Ventre

In June of 2013, I took a vacation to New Mexico. I had never been to the Roswell Museum and thought it was about time. The museum was larger than I expected and had a first class research library on UFOs. I did think the museum needed some updating with interactive displays and posters instead of having newspaper clippings taped to the wall. Upon leaving Roswell, I saw a female hitch-hiking at the edge of town on Main Street. I had seen her the day before at the Chinese buffet where I had eaten dinner. I decided to pick her up.

She was carrying no bags which I thought was strange. She wore a western bluish blouse and jeans. She was rather large on the bottom but had a beautiful face and blonde hair. Her eyes were very strange; light gray but bloodshot. She had albino type features. I again thought it strange that someone who was probably allergic to the sun was walking in the sun at eleven am in 111 degree heat. I'm not in the habit of picking up hitch-hikers but I could see that she was not armed. She wasn't even carrying a purse.

When I opened the car door for her, she said, "I have travelled a long way." I recognized this phrase as an old Masonic pass code when meeting. Only I am not a Free Mason. We talked on the 178 mile ride to Santa Fe. She said she was also headed there. She said her name was Sigrun. I told her about my visit to the UFO museum and that I was on the Board of MUFON and their Pennsylvania State Director. She said she knew. When I asked her how she knew, she said, "It wasn't important; probably saw you on TV. What is important is what I am about to tell you regarding the true history of mankind on this planet".

The following is what she told me:

"I'm only going to tell you this once so please do not interrupt me. There's not enough time for questions. In your beginning, it was "Them". It has always been "Them". They have been here since your beginning. They placed the moon where it is to stabilize earth's orbit after earths original moon was destroyed in a collision with a comet. Earth's orbit would wobble and every 26,000 years earth would gradually take a forty five degree change or turn. North America would end up in the Arctic and then migrate to the equator. No other planet in this solar system has a moon orbiting it that is one forth the size of its planet. Earth has had four great ice ages and the moons re-placement stabilized the earth's rotation and created tides and the four seasons in a stable environment. Mother Nature can act like a serial killer at times. The moon is actually four billion years older than the earth and the reason it doesn't rotate is because "They" placed it there and reside there. "They" seed the universe and spread the gift of life through DNA that they have accumulated from other worlds. They can also terra-form planets when necessary. After "They" left, other progenitors came here 72,000 years ago from a planet within this Galaxy. They arrived after your Indonesian Toba super-volcano eruption which killed ninety percent of life on this planet 72,000 years ago. "They" came to re-populate this planet like they did before and after your dinosaurs. A different group will soon arrive right before your Yellowstone super-volcano eruption. They don't care about saving your environment because it will get destroyed and regenerate; always does. A new group gets selected to re-populate after every global extinction event. Your own U.S. Air Force taught a Physics 370 class at your Air Force Academy in Colorado Springs from 1968 through 1970 where the text said they came here 47,000 years ago and that there are three or four different species. You can look it up even though they were off on the time frame; sounds like they weakly inverted the time period. There are human looking, short Grey looking, Reptiles and Insect like ETs. Those are the four types. All life will slowly evolve over millennia but evolution can and should be advanced. Genetic engineering is part of evolution. When you can cure a disease, you do. When you can transplant an organ, you do. When you can advance the species to be healthier, smarter and stronger, you will. If your planets orbit changed and you knew you would be living in an ice age or an inferno, would you genetically alter the species to survive? Wouldn't you prefer to feel like thirty for the rest of your unimportant life?"

"Just like "Cocoon". I said. "But there are no stages of evolution in the womb. Ernst Haekle hoaxed that in the 1880's."

"What does a cocoon have to do with what I just said?"

“Never mind but I do agree that DNA is a language and language is not random like evolution and older languages were more complex than today meaning we were smarter.” I said.

“There are a lot of confrontations between the four species. Neither wants to genocide a planet or species but there are confrontations. Soon you will be faced with moral dilemmas regarding your species with its aging overpopulation, dwindling resources and technical ability to improve the species. Will the United States put its head in the sand while China creates super soldiers? They can already splice fish and spider silk DNA into a soldier and make his skin like Kevlar and not feel extreme cold. The military has contact lenses that act like a computer in your eye which coordinate Intel and night vision. How do you kill someone who regrows limbs, has no remorse or fatigue?”

“I guess you keep what you kill but I want bat sonar so I can sense everything around me at night.” I added.

“As much as you don’t want to do something, there’s always another group that will force your hand. Where will the human engineering race take you? Your government already has the ability to target markers in DNA; age markers, IQ markers, racial markers. Your species has no master plan. You prefer the status quo but war and social handout programs are unacceptable. Human improvement is the only worthy goal. Many times the creature that leaves a planet on a space mission is not the same as the one that created it for the ride. If you have to confront four generations in space with no gravity or if you needed gills on a water world, they can be added. Your singularity will occur on February 14, 2045, Valentine's Day, when the marriage of man and machine will occur on earth." Said Sigrun.

I adjusted the gold cross hanging around my neck and said, "Are there any worlds where the rise of the machines took over and killed its creator?"

"Yes there are a few. It's all in the programming and the hosts DNA. Live by the sword, die by the sword."

I lip synced the music from Terminator, "do-do-do-dodo" and Sigrun just stared at me.

"I'm getting ahead of myself. When "They" came here, you had evolved from chimps and apes into hominids or cavemen. "They" spliced their DNA into the hominids and created the Neanderthal. Then they observed your behavior and development. They gave your body a lifespan of 120 years. "They" live much longer and age much slower but you were created in their image. They did splice their DNA with Cro-Magnons and Homo-sapiens as the experiment progressed. Cro-Magnons actually came after Homo-sapiens, not before. That's the missing link in your theory of evolution. Cro-Magnon existed for only 10,000 years during the last ice age and was killed off by humans. Humans received 226 genes that can be found in no other ancestor on your family tree.

That's another missing link in your theory. You are so different than your ancestors that you pretty much don't belong on the same family tree. A by-product of the 226 genes is that you have more genetic mutations and diseases. That's the result of splicing the DNA of two similar species together. Chimps have 200 deformities, you have 6000. You also have forty six chromosomes while all other primates have forty eight. Because you are the product of two species, you have bad backs, can't be out in the sun too long and your infants heads are too large at birth. "Their" planet had less gravity which made them anatomically different than you. Humans did not walk out of Africa and spread all over the continents. "They" also created the four different racial groups that look so different. It wasn't the environment or diet that caused the differences like your Professors teach. If you look at a globe and follow latitude or one line east or west you will see that it passes through South America, Africa and Southeast Asia. If you all lived in the same temperature then why do you all look so different if evolution is correct?"

"Actually, God created everything, including stars, fully aged and mature. The law of Biogenesis says life only comes from life. But your scientists say the fossil record for apes ends eight million years ago and chimps, gorillas and orangutans also just appear like us yet our genes are too similar to apes for that to be possible! I've also always wondered why the male and female brain operates so differently. Men alternate one side of the brain or the other to solve problems while women use both sides at once with tremendous overlap. Men are more coordinated and logical while women are more social, can multitask and have better memories, unfortunately. Biologists say it is because men were the hunters yet most men haven't hunted in generations and the same is not true of other primates." I said.

"Your differences were engineered in so that each served a primary function."

"Was my son's diabetes caused by "Them"? I ask.

"There is a species here that wants to destroy you. They abduct humans and cattle and create biological viruses to rid the planet of you. They've caused the increase in diabetes, autism and cancer that you've experienced but they can't seem to create the super virus because you have the DNA of two species in you. They target the human in you and the "other" in your immune system fights back. Lucky for you, they are not a highly advanced species."

"Ancestry.com is owned by the Defense Department. I wonder if they are searching for a specific hybrid alien DNA?"

"Yes they are."

"Didn't cattle mutilations start in the late 60's and HIV in the early 80's?" I ask.

"Correct; that was "Them". There is another species that uses the cow as a womb for hybrid births between humans and "Them". The infant is thirty six to forty inches long when born. The incubation period is three months. They then discard the cow carcass and that's what you find. They need an animal big enough to carry this hybrid."

"I guess they use elephants in Africa." I joke.

"They do but the correct question is, "When did human mutilations start?" Asked Sigrun.

"I actually have a friend that told me about human mummifications that were found throughout the country over the past thirty years. The bodies are found in trees and drained of blood. The Todd Sees case near me in Pennsylvania is a good example. Is that what you mean?"

"No, human mutilations started in Whitechapel London in 1888 and lasted for three years. After taking the inner organs and vagina from eleven humans, "They" moved on to animals whose wombs were large enough to carry the hybrid chimera. No human serial killer committed that crime. That's a fact, Jack!"

"But there was no blood with the cattle. Jack left a mess?"

"Did I say it was the same species? Jack was 80 years earlier".

"I never put the two together. Seems to me that any advanced species would've been worshipped as Gods thousands of years ago when they appeared and human sacrifices were common?'

"All of the Greek, Norse, Roman and Egyptian Gods and legends were "Them". The original groups that placed the moon in place and created you have moved on. Others have come and gone. The ones here now are not as old or powerful. The Greeks called them Apollo, Zeus, Poseidon. The Romans named them after the planets. The Vikings called them Odin, Thor and Loki. Poor Prometheus, he tried to help the newly created humans and was bound to a cross and disemboweled with a laser. Laws are laws. He thought he could sneak medical devices and vaccine's to the humans but that wasn't allowed. I'm not sure where the legend of him giving us fire came from. We were already quite intelligent. They were allowed to be in contact with us and ruled over us but no technology was allowed to be passed on. They wanted you in harmony with nature and knew you would copy any instruments you were exposed to. They were trying to create religion and laws and keep your species pure. India was a good example.

"I can tell you that there are many different worlds with different races and forms of government. On some worlds, dolphins and parrots are the intelligent species but they can't build anything of significance. Any society that is burdened with social programs and entitlements will advance very slowly. The elderly who didn't plan ahead and the lazy who won't contribute will drag on your development like an anchor. There is a tipping point with generosity where it becomes an entitlement burden. Socialized worlds take eight times longer to advance. There have always, and will always be peasants until you genetically advance their IQ. You can't cripple your advancement to prop them up. On some worlds, humans are no smarter than chimps and are herded and eaten as food."

"I laugh when I see movies with futuristic cities but if the moon moves two inches a year away from earth, shouldn't it be gone by now? Shouldn't comets have no ice left after billions of years of passing by stars? What form of government advances fastest?" I asked.

"The right kind of Totalitarian ruler can make the quickest changes but the most creative people are those that are free. Look at your history. Did anything really matter for the masses prior to the industrial revolution? Your standard of living barely doubled every 600 years since the Roman collapse. People in 1400 AD were not living much better than the Romans did in 300 AD. All the wars, religions, empire building and treaties didn't make much difference for the average person until you industrialized and got technical. Humans were one of the slowest to grasp that concept. Freedom seems natural but it is the exception in the universe. Most species don't use currency. Your capitalism has to also be cruel in order to survive. What do you do with those that can't keep up?"

I replied, “Give them food stamps. Totalitarian? Russia killed twenty million of their own; China killed seventy million and Japan killed twelve million Chinese. You’re telling me that if we took our elderly that aren’t productive anymore and put them on an ice barge out to sea like the Alaskan Eskimo’s did, we’d advance? If we threw our deformed babies off a cliff like the Spartans did, we’d be better off? I think the moral test of government is how it treats those who are in the dawn of life, those who are in the twilight of life, and those who are in the shadows of life. Once life is devalued, none of us are safe.”

“Very well said and empathetic but you asked the question. Eugenics has its place in improving a species.”

“Somehow I think we are going to discuss Hitler.”

“We will but it was Darwin’s cousin Francis Galton that coined the term eugenics; ironic don’t you think? The U.S. actually had twenty seven states that sterilized the unfit. You now do the opposite by promoting welfare. Your most successful and smartest couples don’t reproduce anymore because they are more interested in their standard of living. Isn’t abortion eugenics?”

“It sounds logical but based on your 72,000 year theory, we have 3500 generations of genes in us and our kids can have any of those traits. That’s why athletes don’t always produce athletic kids.”

"Plato and Socrates contemplated the same along with freedom of thought and punishment of thought but survival of the fittest is the universal rule if you want to get there first and not end up like the American Indians. Your kids are the first American generation that won't end up better than their parents. That wasn't the plan. Can you imagine what your great grand kids will be up against? Think of it this way; it can't be a zero sum game. When you have to take from one to give to another, you stagnate. What if everyone was allowed to play major league baseball? You're in a period of socialism that leads to stagnation and no advancement. There isn't time to stagnate. The bottom dwellers serve no purpose. The real point is that nothing given is worth as much as if it is earned. You can't develop your soul if you are given what you need."

I replied, "I agree with self-worth but I'm not so sure about the future. Technology is advancing rapidly and soon we will have 3-D printers and robotic workers."

"And that is another set of problems. Robots will do the jobs that people weren't designed for but trying to find a competitive hiring advantage over a machine will leave millions unemployed as corporate profits grow. Some planets sold off their unproductive workers as slaves like your African tribal leaders did 400 years ago to the slave traders. Some moved on to a neighboring planet for a new start and left the unproductive behind. Some just killed them."

"Soylent Green." I said.

"I don't understand."

"Soylent Green was a 1960's Charlton Heston movie where we were out of food and everyone ate Soylent Green. "Soylent Green is people" was the way the movie ended."

"That's prophetic, was it in that stupid 2012 Prophecy book that you wrote?"

"That was a sci-fi book. Do you know the difference between fiction and non-fiction?"

"Yes I do." Sigrun said.

"Then which one is real, fiction or non-fiction?"

"Non-fiction of course. Now let's start with Egypt. There are two Egypt's; one inherited its knowledge from "Them". In 8,000 BC "They" interacted with the Pharaohs and some of "Them" were Pharaohs who cut and levitated large stones for the Pyramids. They inscribed the story of their civilization on the gold cap of the large pyramid at Giza but your people stole the gold. Prior to the Great flood of 8,000 BC, the ETs warned some humans of an impending disaster and some humans took their ships out to sea with live stock in them. Noah was one of those that were warned. The ETs observed as the vast pools of water broke loose in North America from the melting of the Ice Age and sea levels rose eighty feet and caused huge tsunamis over the course of a few weeks. Advanced civilizations like Atlantis on islands and archipelagos were completely destroyed along with all coastal areas. All rivers swelled and over flowed. Dinosaurs were still alive at that time and walked with Adam but the Flood drowned them all. That's why you find so many fossils buried not far below the surface and some with meat still on the bones. Flood waters rushed past the Pyramids and left water lines. Your archeologists seem to want to insist that the pyramids were built in 2500 BC but they weren't. I can spend all day talking about the Egyptians. That was grand experimentation froth with genetic engineering and grand construction projects. Those were the days.

"They left many carved records so that their place here would last. The only record of your existence that would last is Mount Rushmore since it is carved into granite. One of the oldest temples "They" built is in Bolivia at Puma Punku. It was created 17,000 years ago and the stone blocks are three times larger than anything used in Egypt. You can't lift those today with your machinery yet your archeologists just ignore the facts and say that they were quarried fifty miles away, floated down river on rafts and rolled into place up a mountain using logs and sand. And no one questions that explanation!"

"I've never believed that theory. I always thought Fallen Angels built them for human sacrifice. But the Flood took place 4350 years ago and the Tower of Babel was 200 years later. There were 950 people alive then because people lived longer and could have babies for hundreds of years. If Egypt is as old as you say, there would've been a billion people there. At 2.5 children per family, it would take around 6000 years to equal our present population. The Ice Age started 4200 years ago and ended 3600 years ago and not 10,000 because we did not build any major cities that far back. Atlantis was destroyed 3600 years ago from the rapid ocean rise and the water lines on the Pyramids prove they were built right before the end of the Ice Age. I think science has it all wrong; the dating of the Ice Age and that we are evolving forward instead of backward. But I want to know what caused all the rain for forty days?" I ask.

"Venus was a large comet that crossed close to earth. We passed through its tail for forty days causing torrential rain which caused the pools of ice-age water to overflow. Venus went on to nearly strike Mars but it inadvertently ripped Mars' atmosphere away and the planet burned up in the Suns solar radiation. Venus got caught in the Suns gravity and became a planet. Venus is the only planet that spins west to east."

"I read that earth had a canopy of water in the atmosphere which shielded us from solar radiation and it took 40 days to collapse. Is the face on Mars a real structure?"

"Yes, it was built by "Them" but they abandoned the planet and moved their way station to your moon and a tenth planet that is on the opposite side of your sun and has the exact same orbit as your earth but is never seen when they calculated the near miss. Mars had been habitable for many centuries same as earth. It was a mirror planet to earth. "They" started with Mars which was more like their home planet."

"So in 1992 when the Mars Observer probe lost transmission over the "Face", it was a cover-up?"

"Correct, but "They" don't care if you discover the "Face". They are curious about your reaction. What country has the most Pyramids?" Sigrun asked.

"Egypt."

"Wrong. Egypt has 150; Central America has 1000."

"I was taught in school that we were still cave men in 10,000 BC. How could we have created these structures without help?"

"You are probably familiar with the epic of Gilgamesh but did you know that it took place at Baalbek Lebanon which is the site of another temple whose stones weigh nearly 1000 tons each. That site was built by Gilgamesh as a temple to appease the ET Gods."

"Yes, didn't the epic describe a humanoid that the gods created to stop Gilgamesh from exercising his "Lords right" to sleep with brides on their wedding night prior to the husband? This was the same rule that prompted Wallace of Scotland to rebel against the King of England."

"Who?" Sigrun asked.

"Mel Gibson in Brave Heart."

"They" created or engineered Enkidu to teach Gilgamesh honor but Gilgamesh was half ET and half human just like Hercules. There is a quote in your Bible that says, "The sons of God observed the daughters of man and liked what they saw and took them as wives". This refers to the Nordic race mating with humans which spawned Gilgamesh and Hercules and other gods and demigods of old. Enkidu ended up failing because he bonded with Gilgamesh and Enkidu was poisoned by the ETs.

"In Samaria Iraq in 6000 BC The ETs dictated their history and taught the Sumerians to record the history on cuneiform stone tablets. They identified themselves as the Nephilim. They gave the Sumerians laws and a written language. In India in 6000 BC, Kings and Dignitaries were flown to Peru and other locations in space ships that they called Virmana and the natives carved the Nazca lines to signal the ships. A war erupted between the ETs over the control of humans and a nuclear exchange took place in Mohenjo-Daro. Some humans were too close and were turned to pillars of ash. Many ETs left earth after what they had done and only a few stayed behind. They spread out to different continents. Have you ever read the Mahabharata?" Sigrun asked.

"I know of it; it described the original "Star Wars". I know when asked about the first detonation of an atomic bomb, Oppenheimer quoted from the Mahabharata and said Americans didn't detonate the first atomic bomb on earth. It's an epic poem eight times longer than the Iliad and Odyssey. Unfortunately, we are not exposed to Eastern literature. It clearly describes a nuclear exchange as you've said and it has blue prints for flying craft and a flight manual. I know we found radioactive skeletons in the detonation area. It spoke of using red mercury to power the craft."

"Correct but did you know there are English words found in the 3500 year old book? Let me tell you more about Egypt. In 1400 BC, the remaining ETs genetically engineered the combination of humans with bird and animal heads in order to control a restless public. These creatures were nine feet tall and were worshipped as God's. That's what I call crowd control. They instructed King Akhenaten and Queen Nefertiti to eliminate all worship of multiple Gods and to only worship one God; their God. They told Nefertiti that she was their child which was why she possessed the same elongated skull as they did. In 1300 BC, many ETs were Watchers from a distance; Mount Olympus and Mount Sinai. The Egyptians enslaved more and more people for their building projects as they tried to emulate the master ET builders. The ETs selected Moses to lead the slaves out of Egypt. The

Pharaoh wouldn't allow it and the ETs introduced and spread small pox. This is the origin of the plague's that resurface years later. Moses was allowed to leave with his people and the ETs parted the Red Sea trapping the Egyptian chariots and soldiers. "They" provided manna or food for the exodus. They gave Moses laws to live by."

"What happened at Jericho?" I ask.

"After Moses' death, Joshua took over. Joshua was a hybrid. During the attack on Jericho, Joshua commanded that seven Priests blow trumpets which really masked the sound from the vibration weapon that Joshua was given and carried in an Arc and used it to collapse the two rows of thirty foot high and six and twelve feet deep walls. You probably also know that Elijah never died but was taken to Heaven. Where do you think he actually went? In 1200 BC, the ETs sent another hybrid to live among the humans named Samson. He was betrayed by a female and tortured after showing off his great strength and killed as he caused a temple to collapse."

"What about the Great Wall of China?"

"That was started in 700 BC to keep the ETs out. Some ETs decided to adopt local customs and ride on horseback instead of being seen using their craft. The 5500 mile wall was meant to keep "Them" out."

"I guess you're going to tell me next that a UFO caused the Tower at Pisa to lean?"

"Actually, it did." As Sigrun nonchalantly explained our history, "All of the rock cave drawings and petroglyphs were of "Them". All of your art started as a tribute to them. The Wandjina petroglyphs of Australia; the Utah Sego Canyon cave drawings; the Abydos Egyptian temple carvings of flying craft are all over 7000 years old. There are cave paintings in Tanzania of flying discs that are 30,000 years old."

"What if Satan planted those cave paintings and petroglyphs to trick us with the deception of aliens who are demons? When the Rapture, occurs, we'll be told that aliens took the Christians and not God. What if we are being pre-conditioned?"

Silence and no response.

"I remember seeing the "2012" movie where they brought two of every species on board a ship to save them kind of like Noah. I couldn't help but wonder why they didn't just show vials of DNA in the movie with each species. We have the Frozen Arc Project in the U.K. for that very purpose."

"They absolutely bring the DNA from planet to planet. That would've been a forward thinking idea for the movie but it looks visibly more pleasing on screen to bring the animals on board."

"I have heard sometimes it rains frogs or fish. How does that happen?"

"Many of "Their" craft are stealth to your eyes. When "They" harvest, they collect a particular species and dump the remainder when "They" have enough. Same as your fishermen with their nets."

"That would explain why it is one species that rains down and not a collection as if swept up by a tornado." I said.

"In 1000 BC, the ETs interacted with the Greeks and identified themselves as Zeus, Apollo and Athena. Ezekiel was awe struck by the sight of the craft in 593 BC and started to form a religion and word of mouth spread. In 332 BC, Alexander the Great tried to cross into India and was repelled by two UFOs that swooped down at his troops and scared the horses and elephants. Alexander turned back. These were the same craft I mentioned earlier flying from India to Nazca Peru. "They" had a liking for India and really influenced their culture with the Hindu religion. Gandhi was one of "Theirs". Like Jesus, he taught passive resistance. Did you know that Hindu and Sumerian are both 8000 years old and were the first religions and written language that your modern human had?"

"Yes and computers have returned us to a common language but Buddhism doesn't believe in a God. Alexander was tutored by Aristotle and died at the age of thirty seven. I wonder why those same UFOs turned on him after they helped him at the Siege of Tyre a few months earlier. The craft fired a pulse weapon at the wall of Tyre and caused it to collapse and the Greeks to enter and win the battle?" I said.

"That was a different group of ET. They were probably setting up the attack on India but Alexander's troops fled when repelled."

"In the movie "The 300" how did 300 Spartans hold off 250,000 Persians in 480 BC?"

"The goal was to save Democracy. Leonidas was a hybrid as were many of his Spartans. They had to stop Xerses and were aided by "Them". The spread of Democracy was the real long term goal but the Persians were actually the freer society. They outlawed slavery and had a volunteer army unlike Greece."

"The way I remember it, Xerses gave himself to the devil to become a God-King and transformed into an eight foot tall tyrant after Themistocles killed his father King Darius at Marathon. But yes, saving democracy was the goal and God helped the Greeks win the naval battle at Artemisia. . . . I've always heard mythology of ancient monsters and creatures like the half man-bull called Minotaur and the half man-horse called Centaur, are you saying that they were all genetic experiments?"

"Yes, to scare and control ignorant humans. You live in the illusion of reality."

"Which were your favorites?"

"I liked the half lion-eagle Griffin and Cerberus the three headed dog. I never liked the half humans because you were a semi intelligent species for show only."

"How did they get the snakes on Medusa's head?"

"That was Greek mythology. Homer didn't write that one but another story teller did but the Kraken was real. Your seas were full of giant creatures that "They" re-created. Homer was one of "Theirs" and his works were the basis of Greek and Roman education and literature. His works set the tone for moral behavior and laid the basis for your democracy. No one knows when he was born or where he lived because he was one of "Theirs" but his stories of Troy and Atlantis were real." Sigrun said.

"The Greeks believed humanity was the pinnacle and submitting to God was weakness. They took the biblical figures and gave them different names. Adam and Eve became Zeus and Hera or later known as Athena. They brought humanity enlightenment symbolized by lightening. They initially had two sons just like Kane and Abel except Ares becomes a hero as the Greeks twist everything around. Noah's son Ham became Hercules. So tell me, was Hercules a hybrid too? That would explain his strength and tales of conquest."

"Yes, he was about three times stronger than you. He did fight the chimera you call Hydra. It was genetically engineered and uncontrollable. Hercules had to cut off its heads. "They" sent Hercules on many tasks to prove himself. He went with Ulysses to recover the Golden Fleece which was really an article of ET clothing that was stolen. The cloth was indestructible. "They" didn't want any proof linked to the fact that they were here and he was tasked with recovering it"

"So why don't "They" do that now; bring back creatures or create new ones and just release them in cities and watch the panic and response?"

"They could but you have progressed to where you could and would easily kill them. The game is to wait just twenty more years till you can create your own chimeras and "They" observe what you do. It is coming, believe me."

"Did "They" have anything to do with the Rosetta stone?"

"Yes, "They" have always left clues. The stone has a third translation from hieroglyphs to Greek to "Their" language but you haven't discovered that part yet. Your Morse code was also you accidentally picking up "Their" transmissions."

"So was Adam being a gentleman when he blamed Eve?"

"Why did God create a tree he didn't want Adam and Eve to eat from?" Sigrun retorted.

"To test us, Adam is as different from Jesus as earth is from heaven. Adam didn't sin but accepted Eve's punishment to support his wife."

"Eve wasn't Adams first wife. Lilith was. She had an imperfect soul and she became a vampire, the very first named Semjase. You know Santa is an anagram of Satan." Said Sigrun.

"And God spelled backwards is dog!"

"Satan hijacked Xmas from Jesus by creating the Santa character. Maybe you can tell me where Christmas trees are found in the Bible?"

"Actually Santa is St Nick who was at the first Nicaean Counsel in 325 AD and argued in favor of Jesus and Christmas trees represent the tree of life and knowledge and the balls are the apples that Eve wrongfully ate from. The leaves on the original tree were razor sharp because the tree was forbidden" I said.

"Now that is good!"

I smile and say, "Not to get off the subject but a few months ago, my local news carried a story where there was a horrific car crash. A twenty one year old college student at Seton Hill hit a disabled vehicle in the left lane of route 30 and she caromed into traffic and was T-boned by a pickup truck and rolled into a gully. She was crushed in the car but was still alive. The fire department and EMS were trying to cut her out but she was crushed with the metal but still alive and conscious. Since she was a theology student, she requested a catholic priest who suddenly appeared. He stayed by her side for forty minutes holding her hand and comforting her and finally gave her the last rites. There were at least twenty witnesses to the priest along with four camera crews from local network TV. The priest never appeared in any of the video and live feed on any of the four crew's video. Still pictures from the Fire Marshall also did not show the priest but all the witnesses said he was there. I could see her talking on the screen and her hand was suspended as if something invisible was holding it. What do you make of that? It's haunted me for months."

"I am aware of that case and your phony media invented a Reverend Dowling a few days later to cover it up and said he was the one who comforted the girl. There is a spirit world and an evil world."

"If there is a God, then there is a devil!" I state.

“Gabriel was one of “Theirs”. He didn’t slay THE DEVIL but he did kill an alien leader of a horrible race of sadists. It went by the name of Hobs.”

“Did Gabriel have wings?”

“Yes that species of ET does have wings. You call them Archangels. This is where it gets confusing for humans. “They” did send Jesus to you as an Ambassador and to teach you non-violence and look what you did to him. He was killed only three years into his quest and toward the end he told Pontius Pilot that his Kingdom is not of this world and that the fate of this world depends upon these three words that must be spoken when “His” people return for him; “Calicau, Salisau, Zeezar”. The soldier that speared Jesus on the cross, Cassius Longinus, was one of theirs. He still walks the earth as punishment for what he did. Prior to Jesus, “They” were always trying to teach us. After Jesus, they started interfering and manipulating events. They want us to have civilization and laws. The ETs decided to rarely show themselves to the humans any longer after the death of Jesus and disguised their appearance as animals and creatures they’ve encountered on other worlds. Their role after that was to manipulate and observe the human behavior. Their greatest project has been the observation of religions. Your need for an all-powerful superior being who will protect and forgive you is the ultimate psychology course. Just look at Muslim and Christian. They follow the same God, but one says Jesus is the son of God and the other says he is a prophet and God has no need for a son and both are willing and have died for that belief. They gave you Jesus, Mohammed, Buddha, Confucius and all humans did was completely miss the message and fight." Sigrun said.

"Muslims and Jews follow God but you can't get to heaven following only one third of holy trinity. You have to go through Jesus. So is Heaven a spacecraft or a planet?"

"A dimension." Sigrun said.

"I always thought it odd how prior to Jesus the Old Testament was vengeful and you had to fear God but after Jesus we're taught to turn the other cheek and love thy neighbor. I learned how God offered his son, the second Adam, to defeat Satan; I mean aliens. Maybe Satan lost some of his power to be openly seen and shapeshift after Jesus said on the cross "It is over" meaning the reign of Satan?" I ask.

Sigrun stares at me and says, "In the end, Satan will be turned into a man and all will look upon his dead body and ask is this the man that made the world tremble and his blackened soul will be cast into the lake of fire and he will never harm man again"!

I'm stunned and clumsily ask, "Why do Muslims worship a black meteor that fell from the sky and pray five times a day? They say that Jesus didn't resurrect. I read Pilot committed suicide after what he did. Wasn't there was an eclipse and an earthquake when Jesus died?" I rambled on.

"One question at a time. You don't think "They" can control the weather? Who do you think the two men in brilliant white outfits were that removed Jesus from the cross as the guards stood frozen and unable to move?"

"Wait, if Jesus was an alien or time traveler, why did he allow the Romans to savagely beat him? He could've stopped them."

"It was necessary to sacrifice one individual."

"So Judas didn't betray Jesus?" I ask.

"No, he did as Jesus requested. But Judas created a false flag where he thought Jesus would defend himself and destroy the Romans; but he didn't. The murder of Jesus had to occur to form a powerful religion but it didn't have to be that way."

"Yet I've heard so many times during a haunting or exorcism or alien abduction that calling out Jesus' name deters them. Why does it work if he is not the son of God?"

"I said "They" sent him to you and that he was an Ambassador but he was a very-very powerful being."

"So you are saying there is no God?"

“I didn’t say that.”

“So what are you saying? That we don’t have souls?”

“Some of you do; just the descendants of Jesus and Mary. After 2000 years of reproducing, a lot of people have their DNA and a soul. Same as you have the original DNA of two species. It’s a geometric progression. The rest of you are like intelligent animals. Look at the crimes you commit and what you do to each other. Ever look into the eyes of a psychopath? Then you’ll know who evolved from animals and were upgraded and who was engineered and has a soul. We don’t have time for the God lecture now but there is an all-powerful force. Your bible is a cryptogram; your future is written into it if you can decipher it. Your DNA is too. Your genetic code defies natural explanation and remains unchanged for as long as you exist. That is why “They” put a message in your DNA. What better place to store it? They stored the message in the left paw of the Sphinx and at the library of Alexandria but the Romans burned it. We stored the message in the Mayan Popol Vuh but the Spaniards burned the sacred documents. You humans look to the pyramids for clues; look to yourselves! ”

I pulled the car to the side of the road and stopped and said, “I don’t know of a more important question to ask than the God question. The descendants of Noah have souls because Jesus didn’t marry Mary. Jesus was free of sin or he would never have been allowed to re-enter Heaven. The whole Opus Dei vs the Priory of Sion story was a 1956 French hoax."

Sigrun replied loudly, "Where is your God? What is worse? To believe what is not true or to not believe what is true? You are not the product of chimps and baboons that miraculously evolved into humans. Dinosaurs did not evolve into birds. "They" engineered those changes same as they engineered Anubis, Seth and Horus in Egypt! You descended from superior creatures that have been worshipped as GODs here and on many worlds. Do you really think that ninety seven percent of your DNA is junk? Why do you only use ten percent of your brain capacity? There are those among you that can see the future; can move objects; can remote view, can communicate with other dimensions." Sigrun said.

"Because we lost our *grace* in the garden of Eden. We had those abilities! An innocent Eve was tricked and we lost our spiritual connection to God and the process of aging began. We are a de-evolved version of Adam who was a superhuman with a genius level IQ. How do you think the ancients performed brain surgery and had advanced mathematics for colossal construction and knew astronomy? Humans could live 1000 years and our genes were so pure that we could regenerate and heal wounds instantly. He was as strong as a silverback and could run with the lions and had a psychic connection to God. We gained knowledge of good and evil but the evil is here only to test and corrupt us. Our God is not an absentee landlord who abandoned his property." I said. "I can only imagine their shock. One day they are in paradise playing with wild animals where nothing aged or died or harmed each other and the next, these animals who were their friends like the *Lion King* were hunting them. I keep picturing the shock when they approached their lion friend only to have him turn and snarl and slowly stalk them. How they must've regretted their decision."

"So what is the argument against the bible?"

"That there are no original documents" I said.

"The originals are in the Vatican locked away and they are very different than those that are published."

"Yet they both have the watermark number 7 embedded deep between each page. How did it get there? There were 40 authors of the bible yet each one has the same embedded watermark."

Sigrun is tight lipped.

"I guess it is the book ET's love to hate." I said.

After a pause, I said, "I read once that all paranormal activities were actually a projection of our minds. We actually create the bumps in the night and voices. It's not psychosis but our brains have that under used ability of telekenesis."

"For some, the unexplained incident is created by them. For others it is real and not controlled by them. You all have these latent abilities from your ancestors. You're a dumbed down version of "Them", not an advanced version of ape! One day you will engineer your way forward. You all have the ability to be God-like. That is part of the plan; your destiny if you don't destroy yourselves first! "They" watch your progress and create barriers and opportunities. Because you killed Jesus, you became a science project. You are so lucky there wasn't a different outcome after you showed your true nature."

"I believe I am the ultimate product of the one and only God and that Jesus was his son and our soul is our higher consciousness and you will not change that but I will grant you that genetic engineering makes more sense than evolution but a creature cannot become the Creator."

"Yes you are; but which God? Each galaxy has a God at its center. You think it is a black hole. When the Andromeda God arrives and galaxies collide, your Milky Way God will be no more."

"That's a tough concept to wrap my mind around."

"You are entering the next phrase where, like it or not, you will engineer your evolution. Like father, like son. I will tell you that there will be a time when humans will experience a shift in consciousness away from materialism and towards the next level of your potential. It will be the end of a male dominated society dependent on government and centered on war. There will be a global wakeup call. Time will seem to speed up. People will be compelled to perform righteous deeds and will have dreams or visions that come true. You will hear voices while awake and then see angels. There will be an evolution of consciousness and your psychic ability will increase. There will be a singularity where all people are connected psychically. You will anticipate each other's thoughts and actions and sense impending danger. Crime will dramatically decrease as you will know what each other have done and plan to do. This telepathic capability is the next step in being able to operate vehicles, electronics and spacecraft using our minds. Indigo or Star children have been engineered and born since 1982 by design. They are technologically savvy, question authority, have higher IQ's than their parents. They will refuse to support the government, pay taxes and enlist in the military. This change can come naturally or it will be engineered. On some planets, especially the Insectoid planets, there is a hive mentality. All creatures are connected like one neuron in a brain to the super brain or computer. That's a powerful weapon; full control. There is no dissention. It's like communism without corruption. Now drive. This is not a debate. I've come a long way and there is not time to stop."

I looked at her and knew she wasn't telling me the whole story. Is it God or were we engineered or a combination of both?

Why does she refer to us in first person and also third person as if she is not one of us? I also wondered if she could read my mind and decided to keep driving and hear more.

"So what do we have next; witches, warlocks and killer clowns?" I asked.

"Funny, I hope you are taking me very seriously. I am giving you or can give you the answers to all of life's mysteries; but only if you don't mock me like some Michael Shirmer skeptic!"

"I didn't mean to offend you. I have a dry sense of humor. Please continue but first, I'm still stuck on the soul."

"All life comes from life. It is not magically created from nothing. You are getting into areas that I can't fully explain. What happens on earth is a pale reflection of reality. You live from lifetime to lifetime."

"Jesus died for our sins and we only get one shot here but I've always felt that reincarnation made the most sense. What point is there to dying young? One time at work, I signed a document with a totally different name than mine. I wrote the name Jack and then stopped myself. I wondered if that was my name in a past life. When I lived in Oklahoma, there was a heinous crime committed on an eight year old boy. He was tied to a tree and his eyes were popped out with a spoon and his penis was skinned with a razor. I always said whoever committed that crime will pay in the next life." I said.

"Yes he will. His next three lives will be rough. You are supposed to learn from each life and advance. That is why some people are so wise. Near death experiences are real and sometimes you can remember past lives. When a soul enters an infant it loses itself in the undeveloped brain. I know when you die your soul wonders for three days in Sheol before a loved one guides them to the life review."

"That's why Viking's wanted a good death."

"They should've been more concerned about a good life."

"Do some souls advance to the point of not having to return?"

"Yes, some become almost God-like. Like your God but become angels. You are a young species. We keep trying to mold you like clay. What do you think happens after a billion years? You can become pure energy and thought. You can terra-form a planet like this one in six days. Those are your Gods. There are a few all powerful and many just powerful and they do fight sometimes."

"Maybe God moves at the speed of light so his day is equal to thousands of days here on earth? Or maybe one day equals

1000 years and it has been four days from Adam to Jesus and two days from Jesus to today and that the end times are ready and we will then have one day of peace. I also read that angels are always male and can take a life."

"They are and can but they should never be worshipped."

"We're too busy worshipping the creation and not the Creator. Do suicides get punished?" I ask.

"No, sometimes sacrificing your life is viewed the same as a soldier or fire fighter running into a burning building to save someone. Suicide takes strength not weakness. Mental illness is not held against you. Many of the people in your asylums figured out the truth about life but couldn't get their minds around the concept and went insane. Even to me, the concept of Hell would be cruel and unusual punishment."

"The older I get and the more I learn, the less I fear the shadow of death but if you side with Satan, you go to his residence which is cold not hot or wonder the earth as ghosts. Where is the arc of the covenant buried?"

"In an underground maze at Oak Island, Nova Scotia. The Templars put it there with help from Hollow Earthers. They built the Roslyn Chapel in Scotland as a diversion but the Arc contains something unexpected; the scroll of *Goetia*. Drinking from the chalice can cure any ailment but the spell of *Goetia* can control angels and demons like a genie's lamp. Let's continue the post Jesus lesson since "They" changed their approach to humans AD or after Jesus' death. In 312 AD Constantine saw a UFO with a cross on it and was inspired by it and wins the battle that solidified Catholicism as the official religion. That was huge for the modern world. The ETs knew to be there and inspire the winning side. Remember, they want you to have religion and laws and peace but the experiment is to see how you react. Most everything that happens in life is a test."

"I don't want any more of that old time religion. Is the cross also their sign?"

"Yes. You were created to be the heir of the universe if you can pass every test, you will have dominion."

"Well I guess we failed since that lead to the Dark Ages after the fall of Rome."

"Rome had its 700 year experiment as a Republic and was named and founded by Romulus and Remus the sons of ET hybrid Hercules. Most Americans think they live in a Democracy but it is a Republic; sad that they don't know the difference. The best argument against a Democracy is to have a five minute conversation with a voter. Rome had a Constitution but they ignored it after they killed our beloved Caesar in 45 BC. He was one of "Theirs" and one of "Their" greatest examples of what could happen under the rule of law. Laws became meaningless to the Emperors. They extended their terms, devalued their coins by putting less silver in them, bought votes by subsidizing grain, olive oil and pork. Anyone could line up for handouts prior to an election. They tried wage and price controls as debt grew with the expansion of the empire. Empires do crumble and you now face the same threats. We will talk soon about Hitler and the U.S. and China."

"Do you know of the story of Perpetua? I asked.

"No".

"Perpetua was the first female martyred in the "games" as a Christian in 203 AD. She was 21 and was imprisoned in Carthage for not renouncing Christianity. Her child was born in prison and taken from her. She was told it would die without its mother's milk if she didn't renounce Jesus. She said she could no sooner renounce Jesus than to say the chair in the room was not a chair. Perpetua was gouged in the arena by a bull and then slain by the gladiators."

"There is also a planet that has a worldwide earthquake at 3 PM each year on the same day, your Easter day." Said Sigrun.

I just stared into her blood shot eyes and asked, "What about the Mayans?"

"First let me say that religion tried to control thought and stagnate educating the people. That was not the plan so the Dark Ages of religious rule was a failure. As for the Mayans; the one they called Kulkuchan was a Nordic hybrid. He had blond hair, blue eyes and an elongated skull. "They" introduced blue eyes into humans. He ended up in Central America when his craft sunk at sea. He gave the Mayans their calendar and astronomy and medicine. They made him a God as most human tribes did with superior beings. The calendar matched up with the earth's rotation, nothing more. He told them he would return in 500 years and unfortunately Cortez and the Spaniards showed up and the rest is history."

"It's a shame that religious leaders thought it were better to have ignorant pawns rather than educated protestors. So there was no magic to the 2012 date either?"

"No it just connoted (implied) when the earth did a full rotation due to its slight wobble. I told you the moon was put in place to help the earth from having huge gyrations in its rotation. It's on a 26,000 year cycle which 2012 marked the beginning of a new cycle. Your 2012 book was wrong but a good novel."

"There were a lot of similarities between the Mayans and Egyptians who both originated in Babel and possessed the same knowledge of how to build great structures."

"Did you know that in 1136 AD Merlin the magician was actually a hybrid living in England? He constructed Stonehenge." Said Sigrun.

"Yes, he helped King Arthur and the Knights of the Round Table."

"He helped create the British Empire which was instrumental for America. A French or Spanish empire would've created a different less free America."

"Did his wand have powers like Harry Potter?"

"Who? Yes, Merlin's wand, Thor's hammer, Moses staff, Poseidon's trident and Poseidon's brother Zeus' thunderbolt were all alien technology weapons. Even Pegasus was a genetically engineered flying horse."

"Those tricks wouldn't work in today's world." I said.

"In 1177 AD The Templars were aided by ETs at the Battle of Montgisard Jerusalem where 500 Templars defeat 26,000 of Saladin's fighters. How else could they have accomplished such a feat?"

"Just like the Spartans. You seem to be accounting for every event in history. Are you a history teacher in real life on your planet?" I asked.

Sigrun glared at me and said, "This is the last time I warn you. This is real life. . . . and death!"

I replied, "Relax, here on earth we have a sense of humor and I have an audio-graphic memory so I will remember everything you have said; word for word including the telepathy."

"Good, in 1300 AD a craft arrived in need of human subjects. The Anasazi Indians were taken from their mountain Pueblo's. Like I said, this is life and death."

"It's more than disturbing that you have accounted to me four or five times, that humans are taken; and taken in large numbers."

Sigrun smiles and says, "Four or five? I thought you have a audio-graphic memory?"

"I'm glad to see you have learned to smile. Monkey see, monkey do. Oh I forgot, not a monkey."

"I'm starting to understand you". Said Sigrun. "In 1347 the ETs release the Bubonic plague to cull the population centers that were starving and unproductive. They said "We created you like ranchers, now we need to cull the stock." The result was the Renaissance period. So there is the result of your religious dark ages. It was a failed experiment and now man is released to be creative and to question everything."

"And who did they send to lead the Renaissance?"

"Leonardo da Vinci of course. He thought it was cute to use a mirror and write his codex in idiosyncratic reverse script. Even that confounded you humans for years. He wrote on how to fly and create submarines and detailed human anatomy while at the same time painted the Mona Lisa who by the way was also a hybrid. There is one small 8 x 6 booklet hidden in the back of a famous painting that you haven't found yet. That one will change everything. It has knowledge that he couldn't possibly know as a pure human. Once found, you will realize he was more than human. They also gave Guttenberg the printing press so he could help humanity learn and educate itself. The religious experiment was a resounding failure. Your Renaissance was a grand time just like with the Egyptians"

"If they attacked using a virus, how can we survive it?"

"Only those with tonsils will survive."

"I had mine removed when I was six years old."

Sigrun smiles, "I know, as you can see, I'm telling you this in chronological order. In 1429 AD, a sixteen year old Joan of Arc was chosen and was aided in her battles by ETs after they give her divine guidance on how to defeat the British at the Battle of Orleans. Sometimes they pose as angels; sometimes as demons."

"You know Dan Brown wrote. . . Forget I said that; are there misidentifications?"

"Yes, the Salem witch trials were one such case in 1692. "They" showed their craft to Cotton Mather a few years earlier in hopes of influencing him years later. When they showed themselves as apparitions to those two young girls; Abigail and Betty, they were mistaken for spirits. It was supposed to be a revolt against Puritanism that went very wrong with thirty six arrests and twelve executions. Cotton Mather, the influential New England minister, supported the executions. "They" made a mistake using nine and eleven year old girls. Let's continue with Columbus.

"Your Spaniard Columbus was lost at sea and steered south-west into open water in 1492. He saw a brightly lit USO under his ship heading west so Chris veered right and followed it. He then saw it again hovering in the air to the west and headed toward it and guess what? He finds land. You can look that one up in the ships journal. This was another pivotal moment in your planned history. There is a structure to your history. It is not random."

I couldn't help but wonder if she got that one wrong. Columbus was Italian but sailed under a Spanish flag. I didn't want to question her and expose that I think she is one of "Them".

I ask, "What about the Dogan tribe of Mali West Africa? Were they visited?"

"Yes, the Nommo of the Sirius star system made contact with Egypt 5000 years ago and the Dogan actually migrated from Egypt but kept their history. They told the Egyptians about their three star systems and the Dogan told French explorers their history in the 1940's. The Dogan knew of the bright Sirius star and also knew of the two twin stars that cannot be seen without a powerful telescope."

"Wasn't there a Massachusetts's Bay colony that disappeared in the late 1500's?"

"That was the Roanoke North Carolina colony in 1585. Even the passive Indians were baffled as to where you went to? It was very similar to the 1930 Eskimo village that disappeared where they left all their clothes, shoes, rifles, dogs and dinner cooking on the fire. They were all taken."

"Wasn't there a French coin that was minted showing a UFO?" I ask.

"Yes, that was in 1656."

"Since we're talking about France, what about Nostradamus?"

"Hah, he was high on opium. The Greek Oracles were hybrids; Pythia and Sibyl. They advised Apollo and influenced the Greek wars and insured the spread of Democracy. Let me continue.

"They" instigated the Boston Tea Party and in 1778 in Valley Forge, your General Washington was getting his ass kicked. As a matter of fact he was losing most of his battles. "They" choose and create leaders for you. He saw a green orb in the woods and met with green skinned Indians who gave him British locations on a number of occasions. The Indians are actually ETs. That one is also in Washington's journal. The ETs are trying hard to help this new country with their experiment in freedom. The outcome of that war would affect every man, woman and child on earth. Sometimes you just don't take the bait. We can't do it all for you-you know. Where's the fun in that?"

"Why did "They" choose Washington?"

"They thought he would look better on your currency than John Adams. Let's look at the start of your American Revolution. The 1775 midnight ride by Paul Revere was "Them". Revere was a hybrid. His horse was actually shot by the Brits as he rode. He was able to heal the horse and continue his ride. In 1793, Thomas Paine wrote the "Age of Reason" where he said there was no God, just extraterrestrials. He was exiled by George Washington for ten years. That idiot Washington never realized that he was helped by "Them". Thomas Jefferson allowed Paine to return after Ben Franklin told him he believed in the plurality of worlds. You see, most of your founding fathers were not only Masons but believers in ETs."

"I'm disappointed that I've never seen a UFO."

"Look at the clouds from a plane during a lightning storm. Some craft recharge above the cloud in the electrical plume that occurs."

"What are their craft powered by?"

"Unobtainium." As Sigrun gently smiles.

"Unobtain. . . Oh I get it."

"In 1789, "They created the French Revolution that ended the Monarchies and eventually lead to democratic rule in many countries including your own. King Louis the sixteenth, with the help of his wife Marie Antoinette, bankrupted the treasury as human leaders always do and through the use of telepathy, "They" created the storming of the Bastille by the masses. Queen Antoinette said, "Let them eat cake" and was beheaded. Her head sits in a planetary museum as does the real bust of many leaders; Alexander, Caesar, Napoleon, Washington, Hitler and others. "They" prefer the real thing in their museums. Napoleon led the coup of the government and then ruled for fifteen years. Dictators never last. Again, this is the plan to create the pivotal moments in your history and then observe how you handle it but your world needed help. You keep reverting back to an unproductive socialist system."

"Are there any UFO based religions?"

"You have the Raelians who are basically a sex cult and you have the book of Mormon".

"Don't they have two wives?" I ask.

"In 1830, John Smith founded the Mormons when he claimed an angel by the name of Moroni gave him golden tablets written in Egyptian that Moroni translated to Smith. The book says that God created many worlds with life on them."

"And don't forget Scientology. I bought a Scientology book and started reading it. They state that people are basically good. I closed the book and never read anymore."

"A sci-fi writer like you, L Ron Hubbard, but with the occult mentor Aleister Crowley, founded that group. You are correct about people. Your history is full of abuses of power."

"There were also the Jim Jones and Heaven's Gate groups. The Heavens Gate group committed suicide on the same night as the Hale Bop comet and the Phoenix Lights UFO sighting in 1997. I thought that was interesting." I said.

"Too bad the Governor Symington lied about seeing the craft at the press conference in 97. That would've changed things. "They" have used politicians in the past. On April 14 1865, ETs debated the cause to end slavery and decide that for slavery to end once and for all, President Lincoln must be killed. They said, "We aided Moses and Spartacus and creating another martyr 1865 years ago worked out just fine. John Wilkes Booth was used via mind control to kill your sixteenth President and was materialized up and never caught although your history says otherwise."

"I'm glad you do not favor slavery. There is no greater motivator than Freedom!"

"Agreed, but how free are you? When humans are told something by an authority figure, forty percent of you completely conform and seventy five percent mostly conform even when what they are told is immoral or wrong. Only twenty five percent of humans are free in their thought process. You are a sheeple species."

"I never heard those figures but that would explain Nazi Germany."

"You know "They" were there in 1863 at the battle of Gettysburg. They stood in the white mist of the gunpowder and observed the largest battle in modern history."

"Fifty one thousand men died in three days. Much of it was hand to hand butchery."

“They were also there at Iowa Jima when three thousand died on the first day. It was an opportunity to see humans at their worst but at what they do best!”

“Shame.”

“Your 1871 Chicago fire was accidently caused by “Them” and in 1872 the ice covered Marie Celeste was found in the warm Atlantic waters abandoned with food still cooking and tables set for-dinner.”

“Was it “Them?”

“No I just like that story.”

We both smile.

“Do you know why there was such a stampede in 1889 in Oklahoma with the land give away?” Asked Sigrun.

“Whoever staked their land claim first would get the free land. That’s why some people snuck out the night before and were called “Sooners”.

“They actually saw two craft in the sky at the start of the land grab and they all rode like hell! Said Sigrun.

“In November 1896, cigar shaped craft flying over California are dubbed “air ships” and are seen all over northern California. Colonel Shaw and Camille Spooner are abducted in

Lodi and describe the craft as cigar shaped; 300 feet long and 50 feet wide. That was the start of your "modern" UFO sightings."

"What do they want from us on abductions? DNA?"

"Alien abductions are mankind's oldest story. Life only comes from life. There are many groups but for most, you agree to the abduction prior to reincarnation and your progress is monitored. It is co-agreed. For others, "They" are young ETs and are just here figuring you out."

"I feel like this ET question is a "Trojan horse" infiltrating us for a surprise, a deception. The abduction is similar to a demonic possession where each time they return stronger and there is no choice."

"They have no reason to consult humans on "Their" motives or agenda. Do you know the story of the 1912 sinking of the Titanic?" Sigrun asked.

"Saw the movie."

"Ah yes the movie. Only that wasn't what really happened. The Titanic was switched with its sister ship, the older Olympic. The Olympic had sustained heavy damage the year before and was barely sea worthy but more importantly would not pass an inspection. Since both ships were identical, a switch took place but the plan was to sink the Titanic which was really the

Olympic for insurance purposes. There was a coal fire aboard the ship and they planned to abandon her at sea with the Californian making the rescue. Only a USO, unidentified submerged object, not an iceberg clipped the Titanic breaching its hull and it sunk. The Californian was at the wrong location and arrived too late to save the 1500 passengers."

"They also killed the original founders of the Federal Reserve. I guess DiCaprio and Cameron better return their Oscars."

I couldn't help but keep looking at Sigrun as I drove. She had such beautiful facial features but she was so pale and those gray bloodshot eyes kept making me think she was either a vampire or albino. She was shaped like a bumblebee. If she wasn't such a big bottomed woman I would be thinking "*Fifty Shades of ET*".

"Were "They" involved in World War One?" I ask.

"Yes as in all major conflicts. "They" wanted to end Imperialism and draw the U.S. out of its isolationist shell. Do you know the name of the shooter of Arch Duke Ferdinand and his wife?"

"Actually I do. It was Gavrilo Princip a Serb member of the Black Hand." I said.

"Very good but he was a hybrid assassin sent to start the conflict."

"I'll have to update my *Apophis 2029* novel. Any more memorable battles?" I ask.

"Why are men only interested in battles and weapons? On August 23, 1914, The British were outnumbered more than two to one at the Battle of Mons. The Germans claim angels yielding swords cut down many of their troops and aided the Brits. In 1915 in Gallipoli Turkey, a craft arrived again in need of humans. They took a British Regiment fighting at Gallipoli. On a foggy battle field, the entire 800 man Regiment was gone when the fog cleared. There were many witnesses."

"I guess they don't discriminate among Romans, Indians or Brits." I said.

"Correct, they all taste the same. In 525 BC a Persian army of 50,000 men were taken; in 54 BC an army of 200 Romans were taken in Iraq and in 125 AD in England near Rendlesham Forest, the 6000 man 9th Legion of Rome disappeared.

"In 1917 a craft carrying an engineered plague was fired on by the Red Baron and exploded in the atmosphere causing the Spanish flu. Sometimes you were able to shoot them down. It was surprising though back then."

“The Red Baron was one of Germanys finest.”

“Also in 1917, the ETs made contact with three children in Fatima Portugal and are seen by thousands at designated meeting locations. On a rainy day they gave each of the children a true future event; the first two prophecies were that a Pope and an American President will both be killed to stop them from revealing who “We” are. The third prophecy was that they will cause an asteroid to strike the caldera at Yellowstone which will end the reign of human existence on this planet. Two craft were also seen in the sky by 70,000 witnesses and when one flew low, its heat dried off all the spectators on that rainy day. Of course when the prophecies were revealed by the Catholic Church, they were changed and two of the children died the following year from the alien virus and the third was sent to a convent for the rest of her life.”

“Wait a second. You just said that you will direct an asteroid to strike the super-volcano in Yellowstone and kill all of us! The last time a super-volcano blew, ninety percent of life on planet earth died. And you’re talking about a double hit; asteroid and super-volcano.”

“I didn’t say I would do anything.”

“Don’t play semantics with me! THEY are planning to kill eight billion humans. Are you fucking kidding me?”

"I cannot reveal the hour or day of your demise but it will happen after the Chinese era. I promise you that. There is a season for all species and your time is nearing an end."

Sigrun just looks at me with a tear in her eye. I glared back now knowing that they have no regard for human life and say, "Let me tell you something. We already know the time and day of this event."

"What? You cannot. I would never reveal it."

"Something you better learn about humans is that we are crafty and fast learners. Your doomsday event will take place at 3 PM on Friday April 13th 2029!"

Sigrun is stunned. Her mouth drops and her blood shot eyes open widely; wider than I've ever seen human eyes ever open. It frightened me. I thought her jaw would unhinge and she was going to change into something. She then said, "I guess then there is hope for you all. How did you know?"

"I even know the name of the asteroid that you will use to target earth."

"Which is?"

"Apophis."

"How can you know that? Someone has betrayed their oath. That will mean certain death."

I realize she can't read my mind and say, "Just like Prometheus, there are others like your kind that actually want to help us. We have constructed hundreds of deep underground military bases to ensure the continuity of the human species. The Denver airport is one example. We have back engineered your craft and it wasn't just luck that we can shoot you down. We are not paleo-men any longer. We can learn and adapt and do anything you can. Just give us enough time."

Sigrun just stares out the front window. Her eyes don't blink. I'm wondering if she is sending a telepathic message. She is zombie like for at least five minutes. I keep checking the sky for a craft or expect her to dematerialize. I could kick myself for getting angry and shutting her down but now I know for sure that the three quarter mile wide asteroid Apophis will be used as a weapon against humanity. But who is going to believe me? The last time a super-volcano blew was 72,000 years ago in Indonesia. Nearly ninety percent of all life perished at that time. But we are modern. We have technology and more importantly, we have time. We have nearly a decade to plan. I immediately got an epiphany. Maybe the U.S. debt of $23 trillion was actually being used for judgment day because we already know of this event. It must be. How can the government spend the equivalent of $160,000 per person in the past twenty years unless they were planning for something?

Something they could never reveal. They must've captured one of "Them" and water boarded it in Guantanamo until it talked. We're good at that. The C.I.A. knows everything and if they don't, it doesn't take long to find out. Yes, that's it. We already know. Now sadness comes over me. My children may not survive. How will they choose who lives and who dies? I can't think about that now. All of a sudden the car starts to sputter and lurch and slow down like the engine was about to shut down. The hazard flashers come on by themselves and the horn starts to honk. I need to find out more and say to Sigrun:

"Look Sigrun, I know you're one of them or at least a hybrid. There's no sense playing this charade. There is nothing we can do about it anyhow. Continue your story. I am enjoying it and don't believe a word you are saying. I made that whole thing up about Apophis. I actually wrote a sci-fi book called "*Apophis 2029*". I'm just messing with you."

She buys it. The car returns to normal and she comes back to life but almost robotic and says,

"Alright, that's you're dry humor. I forgot you're a jokester. You almost had me. Where was I? Oh yeah. In 1929, 100 years prior to your Apophis, a map was found in Constantinople. Turkish Admiral Piri Reis drew a map of Antarctica on a gazelle skin in 1513. The map of the land is ninety five percent accurate only problem is that Antarctica has been covered with ice since

4000 BC. The fact is that something mapped the earth prior to the ice age. "They" did! That's where Reis got the map. "They" were trying to facilitate contact on the continents but you were too slow to leave your comfort zones."

I smile and say, "The Reis map was stored in the Library of Alexandria and was drawn 3800 years ago by Phoenician explorers when the sea level was lower due to the Ice Age. Remember, the ice started at the center and spread out. It would take a long time to reach the coast of Antarctica because sea water was warmer back then. The Phoenicians also mined copper in Michigan for Europe's Bronze Age. But now tell me about sports figures?"

"Ty Cobb and Babe Ruth were Hybrids. Look up their stats and compare it to the second and third best players. It's not even close."

"What about Miguel Cabrera?"

"They decided to stay away from sports because it's too high profile and why bring attention to the issue. Then again no one seemed to care when players started to hit sixty home runs a few years ago. You humans are really so simple. The May 1937 Hindenburg dirigible crash was caused by a UFO."

"*Oh the humanity*! Wait, how can a UFO not miss a slow moving balloon? I thought there weren't collisions because they can turn on a dime."

"Even young ETs like to clown around with their new toys. They came too close and nicked the Hindenburg causing the helium to catch fire and the dirigible to crash."

"Well I guess they're not all flown by androids and robots then. What about the Orson Wells panic broadcast?"

"I'm glad you're able to ask questions in chronological order. In 1938, the CBS radio station at the Mercury Theater cancelled their scheduled broadcast and reported on a true UFO landing in New Jersey. That started the panic. Orson Wells was paid off to say it was a staged broadcast. It was real!"

"What about the story of the Dropa stones?"

"That was a race of four foot tall spindly ETs who crashed into the Tibetan mountains in 10,000 BC; a desolate place. They were unable to repair their craft or send a signal. The Ham tribe attacked them. They didn't know what to make of the Dropa. They had huge heads and were really ugly and smelled very bad. They eventually came to a truce when the Dropa offered trinkets and utensils. The Dropa created a cave in the side of a mountain where they used lasers to square and hollow out a cave. The walls were smooth and glazed. They drew a map into the wall showing this solar system and theirs. Your military have been in contact with the Dropa's home planet by using the map. They created 716 granite and cobalt stone tablets that were like gramophone records with grooved lines with microscopic hieroglyphic writing telling the story of the Dropa. They knew the primitive Ham tribe couldn't read the stones. The stones were left as their legacy for a more advanced species to find. They were found in 1938 and taken to Russia for examination and there has been no sign of them since. Do you know the story of Hitler and the hollow earth?"

"Yes I do. Do you want to hear it?" I ask.

"Yes, humor me."

"My turn now, in 1938 Hitler sent his agents to Antarctica, Argentina and Chile to search for the Vril-ya and purchase a swatch of land as a fallback plan for World War Two. Hitler was heavily involved in the occult, astrology and ancient relics and interacted with the Vril and Thule societies. The Thule Society was founded in 1918 and focused on the origins of the Aryan race. The Vril Society was founded in 1921 by a group of female psychic mediums and was led by Maria Orsic. Maria claimed to have met with Aryan aliens from the Aldebaren space system who claim to have settled ancient Samaria. Maria also claimed to be able to channel information about constructing an anti-gravity craft and was in communication with Hitler. The Thule and Vril Societies received official state backing from Hitler in

1933 and in 1942 fell under the authority of the SS. In 1938 Hitler also started his research into the "Bell" project in Czechoslovakia. Testing at this site killed five scientists and all plant life. The scientist's blood solidified and the plant chlorophyll dissipated. In 1945 Hitler ordered the killing of 62 scientists, engineers and prisoners that worked at the site and on the project.

"In 1929, Admiral Byrd was the first person to fly over Antarctica and map it. In 1938, the retired Admiral Byrd was invited to Hamburg Germany to tell of his Antarctica exploits. Hitler then laid his plans for "Neu-Schwabenland" or New Germany in Antarctica. The Germans proceeded to map the continent from the air and discovered areas free of ice, warm water lakes and numerous cave openings. One ice cave extended 30 miles into a geothermal lake. Hitler believed this would lead to contact with the Vril-ya race and started construction of underground bases. A second base was built in the Argentinean Andes. The Germans built eight large cargo submarines that were used to transport construction materials to Antarctica. These eight subs were never located after World War Two. Also gone were 100 German U-boats. Two U-boats, number 530 and number 977, were captured carrying 96 barrels of red mercury, which was used for antigravity experiments as was mentioned in the Mahabharata. Members of their antigravity-disc research and development team were also caught. Juan Peron of Argentina also issued 1000 patterns to Nazi scientists.

“The Germans were on the verge of fantastic discoveries with the Vril Series V-7 in 1945 and needed a few more months to extend the war but obviously lost. The Russians and Americans were then in a race to acquire the German technology. The Americans formed Operation Paperclip where 2000 German scientists, engineers and officers were given immunity and homes and salaries to work for the U.S. Military and NASA. Werner von Braun was the most famous of these scientists.

“Hans Kammler was in charge of these special projects and he loaded his JU390 large transport plane with many special project plans and took off at the end of World War Two. This plane was capable of flying 6000 miles without refueling. Many believe he turned over his findings to the U.S. in exchange for immunity since he was never caught, tried or mentioned in the Nuremburg trials. Some say he went to Antarctica.

“In August 1946, Navy Secretary James Forrestal initiated Operation High Jump, which in January sent Admiral Byrd, thirteen vessels including the aircraft carrier USS Philippine and 4700 troops to Antarctica for a six to eight month mission that lasted just eight weeks and sustained six casualties. In March of 1947, Admiral Byrd was quoted in the Chile “El Mercurio” newspaper as saying to Lee van Atta that in case of a new war, the continental U.S. would be attacked by flying objects which could fly from pole to pole at incredible speeds. Many believe that Admiral Byrd’s mission to find the Nazi 211 base was turned back prematurely by these same craft. Interestingly this Antarctic location falls directly on the South Magnetic Pole."

"And three months later, half way around the world, ETs are seen exiting a cave and a boy finds the planted Dead Sea Scrolls and you also got your hands on the Roswell crash! What a coincidence." Said Sigrun.

"You're right. What a stroke of luck after what happened to Admiral Byrd."

"And in December of 1945, five bombers from Fort Lauderdale took off and disappeared in clear weather. A large Martin Mariner was sent up to find Flight 19. They disappeared also. That's six planes and twenty seven crew members that "vanished". Said Sigrun.

"In 1957, Australians discovered a 16mm film of the German V-7 project. It showed an operational disc craft. The Antarctic Treaty is signed where no military operations in the Antarctic would be allowed until the year 2000. In 2003, seismic activity at Lake Vostok indicated military activity." I said.

"Wow, you surprise me. The Brits still maintain a base on the Falkland Islands that monitors the Antarctic activity. That's why they fought so hard to keep the base a few years back. Actually the 1911 Amundson expedition to the South Pole was also a quest to find the Vril. The only thing that "They" are afraid of is the Hollow Earthers. You see they were here first. Earth was inhabited by two distinct and very different life forms. There have been all kinds of out of place archeological finds over the years; gold chains, pottery and vases dating back a million years; found in coal deposits. There is ample proof that during earths four billion year history that it has been inhabited numerous times. You are not the most technologically advanced civilization to inhabit this planet. You're just the last squatter on this planet. Your cavemen inherited the earth from "Them"; the magical beings. Your planet has always been ruled by Gods and worshipped."

"I guess instead of looking to the sky, we should look beneath our feet. So "They" are afraid? They can be beaten. If they bleed, we can kill them!"

"What is this, some *Predator* movie? You can't fight them. It would be like a calvary charge against F-22A Raptors. We only have time to talk about "Them", not the Hollow Earthers." Sigrun said. "I will tell you that gravity and dark matter are opposites and the Hollow Earthers have harnessed the power of both."

"Wait. You mentioned magic. Tell me about the paranormal world?"

Sigruns face turns paler than it already is. "Yes there certainly is another dimension right around us. There are ghostly forms that move and preternatural things that occupy the space around us. They exist in a different light spectrum; in an unseen realm. That's why you can't see them. The human eyes can only see four percent of the light spectrum. Listen to me. You don't want to invite them in. Those ghost hunters don't know what they are dealing with. Once you let them in, they can steal your soul. That is what they are after. You can go from being a descendent of Jesus to being just a human animal. They can occupy your mind."

"Why do abductions seem so sinister?"

"You are dealing with two phenomena; the ET abduction involving science and the malevolent inter-dimensional abduction for your soul. Aleister Crowley opened a portal in 1918 that let the demons in-in force. They are worse than any ET. There is a battle waged every day for the control of humans. There are times that your lives are totally controlled by things from other dimensions. That is why sometimes your lives go so terribly wrong. You have to be strong willed to resist and stay on the right path. There is a looking glass but trust me; you don't want to go there."

I again think that aliens and demons can be repelled by the name of Jesus and say, "That must be why "They" are trying to advance us or prompt us to evolve. What about black eyed kids?"

Sigrun screams, "STAY AWAY FROM THEM! They are evil and will steal your soul."

I thought to myself that I have had a number of paranormal experiences. This frightened me. My kids have also been touched and it wasn't by angels. I felt a shiver go through my body as I just listened on but asked, "I heard Google and Palmolive invented a headset that could see germs only they were able to see spirits and never marketed it. The military purchased them."

No response from her.

"What about Robert Bigelow and that Skin Walker ranch? They say it is haunted."

"It is a portal to the unknown. There are a few like it on earth."

"I thought it interesting that a hotel magnet started funding UFO and paranormal research. He hit it big in 2007 when he sold his *Budget Suites Hotel* chain before the real-estate crash."

"His goal was always space travel and confronting "Them". He used his hotel money to start his Aerospace Company. He knows "They" are real. Why else would he spend millions and risk everything he owns. He had an encounter at the ranch that he won't speak about. It was evil."

"I'm convinced my ex-wife was possessed by an evil Native American spirit when we lived in Oklahoma. We were happily married but her whole personality changed. She became mean and constantly lied. Is it possible a demon broke up my family?"

"Yes, they revel in evil and hurting families. If there was an abrupt change in personality, then she was possessed. How long did it last?"

"The personality change lasted for four years until we divorced; after that I wouldn't know."

"Were you going to church in Oklahoma?"

"We lived there two years; I don't believe we went to church out there."

"It would've helped." Said Sigrun.

I thought to myself that that was an odd statement coming from her.

"It sounds like that's what happened. How does she behave now?"

"She seems like the person I knew when I was younger."

"Why don't you two get back together? Forgiveness helps."

"I can't. Too much happened."

After a pause I ask, "And Hitler was he an experiment?"

"Yes, and of the worst kind. "They" try different forms of government and observe the results. Rome had its Republic, Europe its Monarchies, religion had its Dark Ages and yes, they tried the evil Nazi state also. It has worked elsewhere. It was a horrible time period. So many died but freedom won out as it sometimes does. There is no stronger motivator on this planet than free will."

"Freedom works for about seventy percent of the people. Some people just won't try or aren't capable." I said.

"You can't please everyone. Just stick with freedom; if you can keep it."

"Didn't Ben Franklin say that?"

"Something similar regarding your Republic."

I smile and agree. And then it struck me. Sigrun! I knew I recognized that name from history. Sigrun was the female that recruited Maria Orsic into the Vril. Was Sigrun a Hollow Earther or an ET hybrid? I dared not ask at this point or the conversation may end once and for all. I thought to myself to use open ended questions and to keep her talking.

"What about Einstein?" I asked

"The bagels?"

“Ha-ha, Albert.”

“He was influenced by “Them”. The Nobel Prize winning theoretical physicist didn’t do it all on his own. “They” actually snuck into his office and corrected his formula so E=MC2 actually worked. That was the basis of nuclear power which would come later. They planted a vision in Albert’s mind of the Nazi’s developing the atomic bomb. He went on to convince President Roosevelt of this threat and your President authorized the Manhattan Project. “They” enjoy the domino effect of history when it goes right. “They” also gave him the Einstein-Rosen Bridge theory for wormhole travel but you did nothing with it. You actually took his brain to study but we got his skull for the museum.”

“That’s sick.”

“They also had to insert Churchill, one of their own, into authority as Prime Minister of Great Britain or England would’ve folded under the Germany assault and Hitler would’ve not invaded Russia but instead would’ve developed the bomb first and he would’ve won the war. You formed four new agencies with the National Security Act. The C.I.A., Joint Chiefs and Defense Department were formed due to the UFO threat.”

Chapter Two

Disclosure

"**I**n 1979, my medical informants provided an extraordinary hypothesis but have since been silenced. A pathologist performed an autopsy on an alien body and postulated that early man, possibly Cro-Magnon, had been genetically altered or hybridized. Primeval earth had become an experimental test tube. This would explain "Their" cyclic visitation, some biblical events, lack of communication with us, lack of hostility and abductions. If world governments have the evidence, then perhaps Man's concept of himself in this world would be shattered." -- Status Report II by Leonard H. Stringfield.

About half way through our ride I had the urge for a cheese burger and vanilla milk shake and figured that Sigrun probably needed to use the rest room. All women do so I figured I'd be the gentleman and pre-empt her. I kept my eyes peeled for a restaurant. Amazingly, in the middle of this desert ride, there is a 1950's style diner on the side of the road. It was white and red striped with girls on roller skates. Next to it was a drive-in movie theater where you sit in an old 1940-50's car that was permanently in place. I wondered where you would park your car when you arrived. I asked Sigrun if she was hungry or needed the restroom. She replied, "No". Since I was in the mood for a tall vanilla shake, we stopped and went inside. I couldn't help but notice how large Sigrun was on the bottom half so I knew she ate something and often. She gave me an annoyed look when I opened the door for her. The diner floor tile was black and white and there was a lot of 1950's memorabilia on the walls. Only it all looked brand new. The waitresses all wore red lipstick and their hair was up in a bun.

I ordered a cheese burger and a vanilla milk shake but the waitress said,

"Don't you really want a vanilla egg cream?"

Actually I did. I hadn't had an egg cream in forty years since I moved from Queens. The key to an egg cream is to use ice cold milk and seltzer. After I ordered, I got up to use the restroom. On the wall above the urinal was today's newspaper. Only it was dated April 5, 1957 and was from Detroit and looked new. The sports headline was about the opening of the new baseball season and pitcher Jim Bunning. As I walked back to my booth I couldn't help but notice how authentic everything looked. Then I stopped dead in my tracks as three teens walked in with tight straight legged chinos, white T-shirts and hair up in pomp. They looked straight out of "*Westside Story*". I wolfed down my burger, drank my egg cream and we headed back to the car. Of course a red "57" Chevy pulls in to the lot. I look at Sigrun and say,

"This is incredible. The newspaper in the restroom had my birthdate on it and I'm a Detroit Tiger fan. Everyone here looks like they are from the "50's."

Sigrun looks at me and smiles as she opens the car door and says, "I'm glad you weren't in the mood for seafood."

Now I understood her power. I change the subject and say, "Do you watch the *UFC*, mixed martial arts?"

Sigrun shakes her head no.

I say, "MMA started in the Pittsburgh area on March 22, 1980 under the name *Tough Guy Contest*. Dana White came along thirteen years later".

Sigrun rolls her eyes and then says, "We started MMA in Greece in 648 B.C. It means "Art of Mars" in Latin for the Roman god of war. This one you will like. It's February 1942 in Los Angeles and eleven research craft of the ETs are approaching the U.S. mainland after a follow-up observation of the Pearl Harbor destruction. When they reach the shore, they are met with anti-aircraft fire and the city is blacked out. One craft is damaged and plunges into the shore just north of L.A. The craft explodes upon impact. The ETs then decide to use probes instead of craft to observe the aerial fighting during the war. The probes are like plasma balls but with a solid structure inside."

"Yes, we called those Foo Fighters but my priest told me orbs, Foo Fighters and balls of light were demonic spirits since Lucifer can appear as an angel of light. I know of this Battle of L.A. We fired 1433 rounds at the craft and the city was blacked out for hours. Six people actually died from the shelling. It was the first time we fired on a UFO, the first time we denied their existence and the first time we used the weather balloon excuse. But I thought General Marshall said we did recover a craft?"

"Correct but the craft that went down off the coast exploded and you couldn't fully recover much; just debris. Well, not for at least five more years until you got another chance."

"So you must now mean Roswell, don't you?"

"Yes everyone on earth knows the folklore of Roswell. Two craft were struck by lightning and went down miles apart in New Mexico. You captured an ET who was still alive and the craft debris was fairly salvageable. "They" didn't care about the craft because the fun was to see how you used it and created new toys. They wanted their brother back though and offered a cultural exchange program. When you took him underground in Nevada, "They" backed off. They don't go underground and they didn't know if the Hollow Earthers were involved." Sigrun said.

"So it's mostly all true then? The craft should be in a national museum!"

"Yes, that one is very accurate. Let's back up a little. I'm not done with your World War Two yet. In 1944 in Loreto Italy, U.S. and German troops were firing at each other when both sides saw a UFO and both groups fired at the UFO. It was the only time the Americans and Nazi's were on the same side. In 1946 Sweden, again the craft are flying north to their base and are spotted on numerous occasions and are called "Ghost Rockets". That's what you called them.

"Now back to Roswell but a few weeks earlier in June of 1947 while flying in formation, one of their craft experienced propulsion troubles over Maury Island and had to discharge fuel. The spent fuel struck a boat below it. Three days later a pilot by the name of Kenneth Arnold saw the craft flying in formation over Mount Rainier and he said they look like half saucers. That was the origin of the term flying saucer. Also, the Ourang Medan vessel was found off the coast of Indonesia and the crew was found to be frozen. "They" had nothing to do with that; probably paranormal." Said Sigrun.

"Actually John Martin of Dallas first used the flying saucer term in 1878". I said.

We finally come up on another car on the highway; the first one we've seen the whole trip. There is a bumper sticker on the back that reads, "Do you get this close to God?"

"Did "They" have anything to do with Pearl Harbor?"

"They needed to draw America into the confrontation and end its isolationism. Otherwise, the American century wouldn't have happened and Hitler would've won."

"Which "They" are we talking about? This conversation is like having multiple personalities."

"There were two groups of ETs then supporting each side and humans were caught in the middle as pawns. Fascism involves control by one leader where the state is everything and individuals are nothing. The Insectoids were helping Hitler."

"Because they have a hive mentality and have one leader?"

"Correct."

I looked into Sigrun's eyes and thought to myself that I know her but we've never met. She's like a vague memory or dream. I said,

"You know, you're not a bad looking woman."

"You had me at milk shake. Now let's talk about the 1950's. Astronaut Gordon Cooper saw a UFO over his air base in West Germany in 1951. "They" would always get too close or interfere during the Korean War. They've always observed wars like a Predator during the fighting. Some hope and wait for us to destroy ourselves. Some UFOs were being very blatant and tried to escalate the conflict with China. They would buzz both U.S. and Chinese craft and stop in midair and change direction. They shouldn't have done that. Your conflict with China is just about due now, not then. "They" must've misunderstood the plan. They liked to harass the USS Philippine which confronted them in "46" in Antarctica and the USS FDR which was the first ship with nuclear weapons. They'd also do the same inspection at the Hanford Nuclear Reactor in Washington State which was the world's first reactor. They would scan the ship's crew with powerful beams of light which actually raised the crew's white blood cell count and made many men sick. The military felt provoked. In July of 1952 they buzzed the U.S. Capital in Washington DC two weeks in a row. Every time your military sent up a plane "They" just flew off at high speeds. They were sending a message that there was nothing that you could do. President Truman issued an order to shoot them down if they can't be talked down. That order still stands today. There was actually an air battle off the east coast in the late summer of "52". The U.S. lost almost as many planes as they did during the entire Korean War; 63 over the U.S. and 82 over Korea. You shot some of theirs down also. That concerned them. One disabled UFO had to land in Flatwoods West Virginia in September of "52". People saw it. Another craft came to help with repairs and they both got away. Your government finally took them serious and started Project Bluebook. That was the public view but they also formed your N.S.A. due to the UFO threat."

"I've always wondered why there are more sightings on the fourth of July than any other day." I ask.

"That's because you are looking up that night at the fireworks. They are always there. Did you know that all military bases were assigned a UFO Officer in the "50's"? In late 1953, an

F-89C Scorpion jet was scrambled from Kinross Air Force base to intercept a UFO. On radar, the two merge and the jet and its four member crew vanish. They kidnapped them. They forced President Eisenhower's plane down in 1954 and tried to engage him but were rebuffed by the President. He wasn't going to make any deals to give up nukes with the Russians looming as such a world threat. Ike did the right thing because it was a trick to open the door for the Soviets by disarming the Americans. There is a picture on the internet of the UFO that landed at the base."

"That Captain Ruppelt, that coined the phrase UFO and wrote that UFO book and pushed for investigations, he seemed like a straight shooter." I said.

"Yes, he believed UFOs were real and disagreed with the Air Force brass. They got him to re-write the end of his book in 1959 and say there was nothing to UFOs and then your guys killed him to silence him. Same as they did with Forrestal. Shame, Ruppelt was only thirty seven."

"The C.I.A. or Men in Black?"

"They both work for the same boss. The first Men in Black cases in the 1960's were ETs. Once the Air Force started investigating UFOs, the Air Force personnel would pose as NASA officials with false ID. Then they got the bright idea to pose as Cuban looking ETs with dark tans and dark glasses and black suits.

Remember, Cuba was our enemy back then. The Air Force wanted to create fear and suspicion of the UFO phenomena." Said Sigrun.

"Are the ETs ever mischievous like poltergeists and play tricks on people?"

"They are usually very calculated in what they do although they have caused some problems with close fly-byes. In 1955, "They" taunted farmers in Kelly Kentucky. "They" surrounded the house and appeared at the windows and banged on the roof and walls. The farmers opened fire on them but "They" had a form of force field around them that protected them. "They" would fall to the ground after being shot and then bounce right back up again. This case was featured in your Air Force Physics class in 1968 and was said to be one of the best cases."

"Yes and that M. Night Shamalyan movie "Signs" was based on that instance."

"Also back in the "60's" they were testing your nuclear capabilities and response and wanted to see if your U.S.-Soviet mutually assured destruction policy was true or if one of you would have the sense not to reciprocate. It was a dangerous experiment. They went to your Minot and Malmstrom bases a number of times and shut down the ICBMs or opened the bay doors or changed the launch sequence. One time, they actually started a launch sequence. It was a very dangerous policy test."

"So they were willing to start World War Three as a test? That's fucked up. Why don't "They" try to create a scenario where we decide it is better to disarm the nukes?"

"They have little regard for you. Like I said, you are a science project. If you wipe yourselves out, they'll replace you with a different species but they don't want the environment harmed by nukes. The Progenitors did that after the dinosaurs."

"They're worse than my ex-wife. What happened to this country? The country I was born into has completely changed in one generation. Prior to the "60's", we all seemed to be on the same page. After World War Two, the government, military, media and people all had a common goal. The media was truthful. Politicians were trying to do what was right for the country and people were loyal. It all seemed to change so fast."

"It was the cold war policies that got applied to the media and people by the C.I.A. and N.S.A. that changed everything; Operation Mocking-Bird. Combine that with the eighty six innocent people killed at Waco, Watergate, Vietnam and a UFO problem that they couldn't control and they decided to shut the public out of the truth. The whole Gulf of Tonkin sinking of two U.S. ships was a lie. The most effective way of changing the structure of society is to do it silently. Manage the media and you can change everything; as long as you do it covertly. No announcement is made, just a simple policy change to go from conservative to liberal and break down barriers with the politically correct mix with respect to race and gender and ideas. I've already alluded to population reduction through genetically altered food and viruses. Today, all they do is dumb you down and you are happy. They air a show on tattoos and forty percent of young adults get tattoos. They put inter-racial couples in all shows and ten percent of marriages are inter-racial now. How pathetic you sheeple humans are.

"I know. If you give someone a smart phone, McDonalds and *Dancing with the Stars* they don't care about anything else. Lady Gaga has a better chance of being elected President than Lincoln. I'm glad the U.F.C. is so popular. That's a sport for real men."

"Isn't politics Hollywood for ugly people? What kind of idiots wears their pants below their waistline and then decides to commit a crime and they can't run from the police without tripping?" Said Sigrun.

"People copy what they see. Wasn't Jonestown similar to Waco?"

"No, Jonestown was an experiment outside of U.S. borders in the Guyana jungle where your government tried mind control methods to train and control the group and then offered the 913 people up as abductees in hopes of getting them back and then learning about the ETs. Their minds were going to serve as human tape recorders. Instead, the drugs they were administered turned them into living zombies and when the media found out about the camp, all 913 were killed with cyanide pills."

"I guess a mind is a terrible thing to waste but harder to control! Too bad there isn't a firewall in our heads. Did anything else happen during Vietnam?" I asked.

"Yes, whole villages of people were taken during the war. You also sunk an Australian destroyer by accident. You sent two fighters up to chase a UFO and it led you right toward the HMAS Hobart. When you fired at the UFOs, they veered off and you hit the Australian ship. There was also a rash of abandoned vessels and missing planes in the Bermuda triangle at this same time also.

"You know Lincoln wasn't the only President killed because of this alien agenda. Kennedy was killed also."

"I thought Kennedy was killed by the Mafia or Castro?" I said.

"No, L.B.J. and your C.I.A. killed him. The ETs were proud of him but he was going to disclose the truth. Kennedy requested that all UFO documents be put on his desk by February of 1964 and he sent a memo to the Soviets expressing his concerns that a UFO might be misidentified as an incoming missile and start a war. Your military had been receiving some technology in exchange for not interfering with "Them". Kennedy was going to blow the lid off the ET question which would've put an end to the arrangement. The C.I.A. orchestrated the assassination with the help of Vice President Johnson. Look where the shooting took place and who benefited by it. Johnson becomes President and the secret arrangement continues. How do two bullets cause seven entry wounds? They even set up that patsy Oswald. There were three shooters and Oswald took the fall and was himself killed in Dallas during the prisoner transport. How that could happen in plain daylight with the most wanted man in America? Your media was part of the cover-up and nearly all Americans fell for it. Even the missing eighteen minutes from the Watergate tapes discussed the Kennedy killing and UFOs as Nixon tried to blackmail the C.I.A. Director Helms into helping him get out of the Watergate mess."

"Can I find the memo on the internet?"

"Yes, both memos are out there. The assassination took place only ten days after the memos. But it didn't stop there. When Bobby Kennedy ran for President a few years later, the same fears arose because he was also a card carrying member of a UFO group. Would he tell the truth about aliens? Not only was he killed but also Marilyn Monroe who both Kennedy's mistakenly confided in and Dorothy Kilgallen who Monroe spoke to."

"So that must be why no other President has come forward with disclosure; for fear they would be killed!"

"Correct, they learn the party line quickly after they are briefed on who is really in charge. In your movies, "They" attack and blow up the White House but in reality, they've already invaded and are among you."

"Just like Invasion of the Body Snatchers. I don't know which is worse; to be alone in the universe or not to be. I read the universe may be a hologram and just a reflection from the Milky Way stars. Our Galaxy is like inside a diamond or house of mirrors and all we see is the mistaken reflection of more galaxies"

"Wrong. There are more galaxies in the universe than people on earth. John how old are you?"

"Fifty eight."

"You would've died at five if it wasn't for "Their" intervention."

I felt a chill. "What does that mean?"

"The U.S. and the Soviet Union were going to start World War Three. The missiles were ready to fly with the October 1962 Cuban missile crisis but "They" made their presence known and now you both had a foreign threat. The group that tries to help humans didn't want to see a nuclear war. The realization again that "They" are here stopped the war from occurring. Why do you think Kennedy sent that memo of concern to Khrushchev?"

"We seem to always need a common enemy."

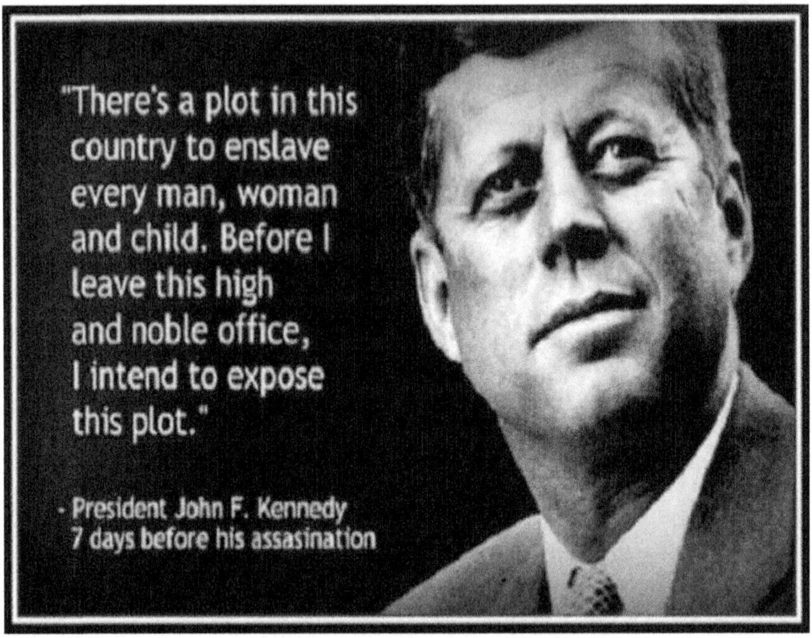
"There's a plot in this country to enslave every man, woman and child. Before I leave this high and noble office, I intend to expose this plot."
- President John F. Kennedy
7 days before his assasination

"Are different species supposed to meet?"

"Depends, some can't handle the truth."

"Like on planet Jack Nicholson?"

"Where?"

I smile. "Was Project Serpo true?"

"You mean the exchange program where you sent a dozen military experts to planet Serpo along with the bodies of the Roswell ETs and they sent you an Ambassador?"

“Yes, it made a lot of sense that Kennedy initiated it. I wondered if that was what got Kennedy killed.”

“No, that was a sci-fi tale. Think about it. Would you want to be part of an exchange where you hand over the bodies of ETs to ETs that you autopsied? Would you want to be part of a twelve for one exchange? That never happened. Why do an exchange when abductions are easier?”

“I remember the 1965 blackout when I was eight and living in Queens New York. You would think that technology would improve but I recently read that there was one blackout in the 60’s, three in the 70’s, five in each of the 80’s and 90’s but one a year since 2000. Why are they on the increase?”

“There is a species that needs the power plants to refuel. They come through a dimension and in order to assume physical form they need power; gig-watts of power. If they can’t get the power to materialize, then they can enter the human mind and control you from the spirit world. Ever wonder why perfectly normal people snap? It’s “Them”. You’re better off letting them tap the power grid. When they enter your mind it is like a virus. Like food poisoning. The host always reacts and it is never good. You can safely assume that that species have visited once a year since 2000.”

“That famous Kecksburg UFO crash took place in 1965 also.” I said.

"Some say that was re-engineered Nazi technology from 1945 that NASA was testing, the old Bell project. We got all that technology with Operation Paperclip. But Kecksburg was really a small U.S. spy satellite that was routinely launched over the Soviet Union. Look up the G.E. Mark 2 re-entry vehicles and you will solve that mystery."

"Why do so many craft crash? You would think they'd be very advanced."

"Why did the Japanese crash planes during your second world war?"

"Suicide missions to inflict the most damage." I said.

"They have no exhaust so the craft are not equipped to spray like your planes with chemtrails. The species that was crashing craft wanted to eliminate humans with engineered diseases. They left after being unable to crack your immune system."

"What about the UFO wave in 1973? I was in high school at the time but I've talked to a lot of people who say there were abductions and Bigfoot sightings." I said.

"That again was another species of humanoid. They had a small window to take soil and human samples and get out. They came up the Mississippi River where it is less populated but then veered east across Pennsylvania."

"Yeah, that's what I heard. There were a ton of abductions though. October 17 had the most in our history."

"Yes there were. Have you ever heard of catch and release?"

"I think that's a fishing term."

"Correct; "They" rarely take kids permanently. Those are the catch and release cases. They want adult samples especially reproductive tissue."

"I remember seeing drawings of the aliens and they looked like the Michelin Man."

"Like I said, just another species that discovered your planet and needed to do their own independent surveys. One species hitch hiked on a comet for transportation. They were only a little more advanced than you but they had to get off their planet and didn't have the propulsion for the long ride. They were able to use the ice on the comet for water, oxygen and hydrogen."

"Where do "They" come from?"

“Some come from fairly close by; 4.3 light years away. You’ll have to look that up. For some of “Them”, it is a forty year trip and for others that are inter-dimensional a four minute trip.”

“Alpha Centauri is 4.3 light years away. Isn’t that where Betty and Barney Hill said “They” were from? What about the Bigfoot sightings that happens along with a UFO?”

“The Hill case was real but that was Zeta Reticuli and they did show them a celestial map of the double star system where they were from. Many creatures from different worlds are controlled or used. The older advanced species do not take humans or like slavery. You have many undiscovered species here on your planet right now. I would say at least thirty percent have not been discovered. There is an earth type Bigfoot who is a Neanderthal-primate and there are others that are brought here on the craft.”

“Why do “They” put implants in people? There is no scar tissue at the implant sight, the body doesn’t reject it and the implant emits a radio signal. Yet the implant moves away from the scalpel and shrinks up and stops emitting a signal when removed.”

“You tag animals don’t you?”

“Is that all we are to them?”

“Yes, an experiment. They have no more regard for you than you do for rabbits.”

"You haven't said anything about the Reptoids."

"They are the Archons. You called them Gargoyles. They have a third strand of DNA but have the same brain as you but they need to dominate and will fight to the death like any reptile does. You have a larger frontal lobe for reasoning. They really are not major players in the universe but they do abduct human women for sex. When cigar shaped craft are spotted, those are Reptoids. They don't use saucer or triangle shaped craft because they can't land them in tight spaces. Reptoids operate like a Seal Team 6 in black hawks regarding abductions."

"I was telling my son and his college roommate about abductions a few years ago and they asked me how many people disappear so I Googled it. There are 250,000 "missing persons" reports a year in the U.S. About ninety percent are runaways that are found or go home but there are 25,000 people who just disappear." I said.

"Yes, and some are children. There are no clues left behind but they are taken. During your Middle Ages, people would blame fairies for the sudden disappearances. The infamous Children's Crusade of 1212 where 30,000 peasant children marched to the Holy land to try and convert Muslims to Christianity and were never heard from again is another example. "

"I thought you said children are catch and release."

"Those that aren't returned are taken inter-dimensional by the dark ones; the evil ones."

"Why doesn't the news report on it?" I ask.

"Many disappear from National Parks and that would hurt tourism. It's the same reason shark attacks at beaches aren't publicized. A lot of times your news is staged or faked anyhow. You do know that? Your media must sensationalize the news for ratings so they stage it after it happened and pretend it is on the spot. Watch the faces of the people in the background. They are usually laughing."

"I heard they first did that with the sinking of the Lusitania and staged the saving of the passengers."

"Correct. The only way that UFOs are of interest to your media is if they can interview the occupants on live TV. Otherwise, you are not interested in testimony; just live interviews and sensationalism."

"I heard years ago that we had an exchange program with the ETs."

"That happened back in the "90's". It was one sided and not the Serpo Project that you asked about. The Americans were never returned. There have actually been a few exchange programs"

"What did their families say? How was that covered up?"

"Easy, you find volunteers whose parents are deceased and are an only child. You'd be surprised how many there are in the military."

"So what went wrong with the exchange?"

"They promised a cultural exchange. You sent seven officers who were experts in various disciplines. They left two behind to teach you new technology and the history of the universe. They gave you some basic information and just "de-materialized" back up or disappeared from your Langley base. Your seven were never heard from again. What we give you doesn't really matter. Others have given you wisdom and technology over the past 72,000 years and you have risen every time only to fall every time into barbarism."

"What did they do with them?"

"Don't know; maybe they ate them."

"You know there was a *Twilight Zone* show like that called "*To Serve Man*.""

Sigrun just frowns.

"What about the moon? Did we really go to the moon?"

"Yes and No. The first two moon landings, Apollo eleven and twelve, were staged in a studio in Nevada by NASA and Director Stanley Kubrick. Apollo thirteen was aborted near the moon due to system failure. That was your first real attempt. You did eventually go on your own; Apollo fourteen through seventeen made it. The first small step for mankind was by Alan Shepard and Edgar Mitchell with Shepard planting a U.S. flag and hitting some golf balls at ETs. Apollo eighteen and nineteen were fully funded by Congress but were claimed to have never flown but they did go on secret missions to the moon in search of the ETs which they saw on Apollo fourteen. You were warned to never return."

"But what about all the astronauts that have come forward regarding UFOs; Gordon Cooper, Neil Armstrong and Edgar Mitchell?"

"You should believe what they say. You know Edgar Mitchell was born in Roswell, don't you? That's why he survived the radiation on the trip while Shepard and Pilot Stuart Roosa died of cancer a few years later."

"Yes, I knew that."

"He is one of theirs." Said Sigrun.

"Mitchell was born in 1930, not 1947!"

"Children get abducted, don't they? Catch and release."

"I read a biologist claims that all humans born after 1947 have a DNA anomaly different than those born prior to 1947."

Sigrun avoids the question and pauses before saying, "If I gave you indisputable proof that UFOs were real, how would you handle it?"

"If there was a worldwide sighting or one that couldn't be disputed, I would hold a press conference and say that I had much to tell the world. I have seen other worlds and other worldly creatures. But based on how the media has failed in its duty to cover this important subject, none of you will be invited to the next airing of the truth. I will do the conference on News Talk 1480 in Latrobe with Hank Baughman since he had me on numerous times in the past to discuss UFOs. No other stations will be invited. You can watch it on TV. You do not get to spin your hat around and pretend now you are the expert. Sorry, but you haven't done your due diligence!"

"Very good, what would you do if "They" gave you their power to terra-form or change matter? I'm not talking about curing all diseases like you would because your son has diabetes. I'm talking about construction."

"I would do two things. I would add 911 floors to the new World Trade Center building in New York City and place a plaque in the lobby that it was built by the victims; overnight. I'm assuming that no one knows I have this power to create. Secondly,

I would construct the Freedom Arch from Newark to Manhattan and at the peak it would read, "*In God We Trust*" and on the other side it would read, "*God Bless America*" both in gold. I would never reveal how they were constructed but I would sit back and watch the reaction that it was a sign from God or the Devil or alien forces. I would sit back and observe the reaction."

"Just like "They" do! I guess the apple doesn't fall far from the tree."

"Wow, you're right. Maybe we are not so different after all."

"You're not. You haven't asked me about the Pope yet."

"Right, what about the death of Pope John Paul I in 1978?"

"Like your President Kennedy, he was going to release the Vatican UFO files which he discovered three weeks into his Papacy. The P2 poisoned the Pope who also discovered serious fraud and embezzlement issues."

"I always thought it was bogus that no autopsy was performed and no reason was given why the Pope's emergency alarm was activated at 9:30 pm and never responded to. Is there any connection to the attempted assassination of Pope John Paul II three years later?"

"Are you familiar with the first secret of Fatima?"

"Yes that World War One would end soon."

"No, that a Pope would be dressed in white and covered in blood."

"I thought that was the third secret?"

"Do you want the truth or what you've been told?'

"Continue."

"I have one other lesson on the Vatican that I'll tell you later. You know there's also an effort to suppress pilots from reporting what they saw. In 1986 there was a UFO flagging Japan Airlines flight 1628 over Alaska and the pilot reported it and was grounded. They were monitoring a passenger on board but even more importantly, the F.A.A. had it on radar and F.A.A. Safety Chief John Callahan documented the case and was asked to brief President Reagan. The C.I.A. then swore him to secrecy and said the meeting never occurred. He went public years later"

"Who were they tracking?" I ask.

"It doesn't matter now, she passed away. You know they took out your Columbia Space Shuttle in 1986. That was not an "O" ring breakdown"

"Why?"

"Payload, sometimes you bring things up there that are dangerous to "Them". You had lab tests on board that would've created a virus harmful to "Them" You also do a lot of bio-virus work at Plum Island, Porton Down and the Dugway Proving Ground but mutations are different in space."

"I'm surprised "They" haven't taken those locations out. Did "They" have anything to do with tearing down the Berlin Wall in 1991?"

"No, you finally did that all on your own. I actually thought that with Reagan and the fall of the Soviet Union that "They" might stick with the United States model and not switch to China but they were too dissatisfied at how far from your Constitution you have fallen."

"What about those two pilots; Mantell and Valentich?"

"Both pilots got too close to the craft. Valentich's engine gave out and Mantell ran out of oxygen as he climbed too high. Unlike Star Trek, that species didn't have tractor beams to rescue the craft."

"Were the good Nordics in Star Trek portrayed by Kirk or Spock and the bad Reptilians portrayed by the Klingons?"

"Yes, very astute of you."

"Any other famous plane crashes?"

"Yes, your J.F.K. junior was about to write a story in his *George* magazine linking President Bush to UFOs when he was in charge of the C.I.A. so your guys took his plane down along with Commerce Secretary Ron Brown's plane because he was about to go public with UFO documents. *TWA flight 800* over Long Island and *Pam Am flight 103* was shot down by a UFO because of the cargo they were carrying."

"Do you know that I almost got on *Pan Am flight 103* when I was working for U.P.S. in Europe? I tried to change my flight and come home a day earlier but it would've cost too much so I didn't."

"That wasn't the only reason you didn't take that flight." Said Sigrun with a very serious stare into my eyes and then says, "Your military now warns "Them" off by leaving those chemtrails in the sky when you are flying an important payload."

After a pause I ask.

"With all this evidence, why does SETI search for radio waves when "They" are already here?"

"SETI and NASA are both placebo's; the public view. Humans are so easy to trick; like a magic show. This whole process has been thought through using psychology by your government. They have you looking over here when the real work is being performed over there by the Air Force. Did you know the

Air Force Space program has been funded higher than NASA since 1982? It's public record."

"The Air Force does spy satellites I think."

"That's not all they do."

"Was there UFO activity with the Gulf war?"

"Yes, did you know that area of Iraq was the original Garden of Eden where many original genetic experiments took place? In 1991 there were many sightings of bright greenish glows in the sky. It caused many Iraqi troops to surrender. One UFO was shot down by a coalition of war ships from the U.S. and the U.K. The UFO buzzed two British ships and three U.S. and all five war ships fired at once and the UFO crashed into the Gulf. The Iraqi military shot one down in "98" and took it to their lab for back engineering. That's why the U.S. invaded for a second time. There were no weapons of mass destruction, just fear of what they may one day back engineer and create."

"So we gave up freedom for security and it was a lie?"

"For your safety. Remember, your politicians think you can't handle the truth. The Patriot Act, RFID chips and FEMA internment camps are all for your own safety. It takes tremendous energy for a black hole's gravity to bend light but space is curved. Earth's gravity causes time to speed up and slow-down in space.

Your Defense Department expends that same amount of energy to bend the UFO truth."

"When did Phil Schneider go public on the Dulce New Mexico base?"

"That was in 1995; fifteen years after he was involved in it. They were Hollow Earthers not ETs. Schneider violated his non-disclosure agreement when he went public and was killed one year later in 1996."

"Didn't he get cancer after being burnt by a laser?"

"Yes, he was lowered into a shaft and surprised the Hollow Earthers and they seriously wounded him. He was lucky they didn't cut him in half."

"Yeah, I remember now. They said he died of a heart attack or it was suicide but he was found with piano wire around his neck."

"Did you know in a November 1980 interview with Cardinal Ratzinger regarding the third secret of Fatima, he said, "When one reads that the oceans will flood entire portions of land; that human beings will die in minutes, and in millions, then one should not desire publication of the secret. Knowledge means responsibility. It is dangerous when one only wishes to satisfy his curiosity, if he is not prepared to do something about his discovery, or if he is convinced we can do nothing to prevent prophesized disasters from happening. "

"I thought you said the third prophecy was an asteroid that hits Yellowstone?"

"You're right. The Cardinal must've changed it to an ocean strike because no one knew of the existence of super-volcano's back then. That Cardinal became a Pope".

"I believe in the end that God will take the righteous off the planet just prior to this destruction."

"Maybe the aliens will just remove those who don't conform to their new religion!"

I just stare at Sigrun who just revealed a truth.

"More importantly, your Western society is rapidly changing. Compare society to ten or fifteen years ago. Your young people are all high tech and gadgets. Some believe that there will be a shift in our consciousness away from materialism and towards the next level of your potential. It will be the end of a male dominated society dependent on government and centered on war. There will be a global wakeup call. Time will seem to speed up. People will be compelled to perform righteous deeds and will have dreams or visions that come true. They will hear voices while awake and then see an angel. There will be an evolution of consciousness and our psychic ability will increase. There will be a singularity where all people are connected psychically. We will anticipate each other's thoughts and actions and sense impending danger. Crime would dramatically decrease as we would know what each other have done and plan to do. This telepathic capability is the next step in being able to operate vehicles, electronics and spacecraft using our minds. Indigo or Star children have been engineered since 1982. They are technologically savvy, question authority, have higher IQ's than their parents. They will refuse to support the government, pay taxes and enlist in the military. Your young people are all about self-improvement and are marrying later and having cross gender and cross racial experiences. Your kids think totally different than you."

I loved the way she changed subjects and segwayed into a different topic. It seemed odd that she repeated word for word something she had said an hour ago. I hope she's not short circuiting.

"You're right; they break up and get divorced via email. The new saying is "all my exes live in text-'s."

"They don't like face to face confrontation." Sigrun said. "That's a regression."

"Yeah, I still say Bloody Mary three times in the mirror on Saturday nights and one of my exes appears."

"What?"

It's interesting that she never heard of that urban legend.

"What about those Gulf Breeze UFO sightings from 1987? Were they real?" I asked.

"Yes and no. Ed Walters saw a UFO and photographed it but he was never abducted. He made that up about the blue light and creatures. He got caught up in the hype and embellished it a little; too bad. He did pass a polygraph regarding the UFO but added the abduction later."

"And that Stan Romanek guy?"

"Fraud, he had a friend hold up a prop outside the window and filmed it. I can't believe how gullible you people are. His wife believes him. He should take a polygraph like Travis Walton did."

"Yeah, Walton passed five polygraphs. His was the real deal." I said.

"It was, except "They" didn't try to harm him. He got it wrong. He got too close to the craft and tried to touch it and he got hit with a static charge. It damn near blew him across the forest. His heart stopped. They retrieved him and resuscitated him and saved his life. It was an ambulance call not an abduction. He didn't realize it at the time but he does now and Hollywood exaggerated it as usual."

"Are ETs harmful to touch?"

"Some are toxic. Two good examples are the Coyame Mexico case in 1974 where four Mexican soldiers died extracting dead ET bodies from a crashed UFO and the Varginha, Brazil case in 1996. Local teens stoned the ET to death and when the fire department showed up, an officer lifted the creature into the ambulance. A few days later the officer died. The bodies of the ET and officer were transported to the U.S."

"How does the U.S. get priority on foreign soil?"

"That's why you give $50 billion in foreign aid each year. It buys a lot of favors including first access to ETs or their craft. It's part of the agreement."

"Any truth to the rumor that the World Trade Center was taken down because there were UFO files kept there?"

"No, just building seven. That was a controlled demolition to destroy the UFO evidence. Your government is rewriting history and purging all evidence in their alliance with "Them".

"I thought so since no sky scraper has ever collapsed due to fire."

"You finished the job you started in 1995."

"What are you talking about?"

"In Oklahoma City."

"Terrorists?"

"No idiot, the UFO files. They were stored in the Alfred P. Murrah building and were discovered by A.T.F. agents working in the facility. Terrorism was the cover story."

"Why didn't they just move them?"

"They did move them to building seven in New York but had to blow the Murrah building so it appeared that the files were destroyed. It also helped lay the groundwork for the Patriot Act and taking away freedoms and controlling and tracking all citizens."

"Nothing is as it appears."

"I hate to tell you but the Flight 93 occupants were all taken and that's why the plane crashed. Records show that the cockpit door was never opened after takeoff."

"Why would "They" take them?"

"I told you "They" like to study your reactions and responses. "They" wanted to study the psychology of both the terrorists and the passengers. One day they will all be returned safe and sound and a lot of questions will be asked."

"What about the distress message NASA picked up years ago?"

"That was in January of 1998 and the high frequency signal came from Andromeda. It was from a world only slightly ahead of yours presently."

"Did NASA reply?"

Sigrun-pauses.

"No the call originated at the start of your Ice Age and just arrived now. There was nothing earthlings could do to help anyhow. But "They" responded and arrived on that world."

"Did "They" save the people?"

"No "They" observed the event and recorded the reactions like they always do."

"That's sadistic not to intercede. Do hybrids attend UFO conferences? I attended my first UFO conference in 1999 and had a series of bad dreams that I think could've been an abduction."

"Yes and so does the C.I.A. Both go to conferences to identify experiencers. And yes, you were selected."

"What do you mean selected?"

"You're not just an abductee. You will play a bigger role. That's why you didn't get on Pan Am Flight 103. I can tell you no more."

I knew there was a reason I was drawn into this. I had no interest in UFOs until I was nearly forty years old. I then ask,

"And how about that big case in 2008 and that object in the Baltic Sea they found in 2010?"

"They're not related. The craft in the Baltic has been there since 1800 and no electronic equipment will operate within a quarter mile of it. Stephenville was "Them". You sent a squad of F-16's after "Them"."

"No I mean during the summer of 2008 in Bucks County, Pennsylvania."

"Some were your military; the TR-3B. You've back engineered zero point energy using red mercury. The Air Force flies from Wright Pat Ohio across southern Pennsylvania and out into the Atlantic Ocean and returns to base over Lake Erie. You use the TR-3B now to confront UFOs but what that blond woman in Levittown saw was a UFO dropping probes into the area and taking samples. She's lucky they didn't take her."

"One of my MUFON associates in Missouri told me about strange sonic booms, fish and birds dying in Franklin County, record snow and drought, a record number of UFO sightings, EF5 tornadoes and an M3.9 earthquake all within one year's times in 2011 to 2012."

"Yes, the UFOs were "Them" along with the Bigfoot sightings. Everything else you described is your militaries *H.A.A.R.P.* program. I also heard the boom while at a Tampa Bay baseball game. The announcer even said something about it." Said Sigrun.

"Yeah, I heard that on *ESPN*. I even saw the Northern lights in Pennsylvania. Isn't *H.A.A.R.P.* a military microwave technology weapon in Alaska that can disorient troops?"

"That's one use. It is also for weather manipulation. They bounce microwaves off the ionosphere and it heats and stretches the atmosphere causing weather patterns to change. You actually have six *H.A.A.R.P.* locations around the world in English speaking countries; not just Alaska. It also disrupts the electric shield around UFOs that allows less developed species craft to maneuver in your skies. You have taken a few craft down using *H.A.A.R.P.* but it doesn't work on dark energy propulsion. The frequency used by *H.A.A.R.P.* creates a different wave spectrum that can be used for communication and surveillance also; communications to your deep underground military bases and surveillance of the Hollow Earthers. It is hundred year old Tesla technology. Too much vibration can cause earthquakes and tsunamis. Humans know very little about tone, vibration and frequency. Tesla by the way was one of theirs. Edison tried to hold him back but Nicola was hundreds of years ahead of old Thomas. Tesla introduced hundreds of inventions and deliberately didn't patent them. "They" wanted to see what humans would do with them. Most went unused. You could've advanced fifty years faster than you did but the military confiscated all his work upon his death and couldn't figure out how it worked. You have a better weapon now than *H.A.A.R.P.*

"America really missed its opportunity after the fall of the Soviet Union twenty five years ago. You forced South Africa to end Apartheid. You rebuilt Germany and Japan after World War Two in a tremendous showing of generosity. We were so proud of you. Fifty years later you went from benevolent to imperialistic. What a step backwards. You spy on your own citizens after we gave you a Constitution. You're failing the power corrupts test. For the past fifty years, all military aggression can be sourced to you. China hasn't seized Taiwan, Russia hasn't seized Georgia. China is quietly winning the financial war. Your Federal Reserve owns your media and controls you while the BRIC Nations have moved away from the dollar and back to gold. China is sending millions of dollars and men into Africa and controlling its natural resources. Cyber war and robot drone war is coming if you don't find your roots again. International bankers have drained the world economy. Where do you think all the gold went? There is no gold in Fort

Knox anymore! A Sino-U.S. war plays right into the hands of the bankers who lend the money to fight the war. China will seize Taiwan, Japan, Siberia and Alaska. South America will be the only area left unscathed. You couldn't even occupy Afghanistan. What are you going to do against China? When they were primitive, they fought you to a stalemate in Korea. Americans have become soft. When the Chinese come, they will enslave Americans and occupy this country with 300 million Chinese and you will be done for good."

"We would annihilate China in an "Air-Sea Battle" with our DARPA technology." I said.

"What, no trail of tears like your American Indians? There are dark forces aiding China. We are not the only race. We each get our turn at your history. As I told you before, different forms of government are tried out on your planet. There are at least twenty different forms of government operating at once right now from Maoism to Marxism which lead to Communism where there is no ownership and to Totalitarianism where even your attitudes and beliefs are controlled to Monarchies in Europe which turned into Socialism to Theocracies of religious rule in your Middle East to Democracies of the people which lead to Republics where you vote for officers to Oligarchies where the rich rule. No one form of government works on this world because humans are so unpredictable. Reptoids, Insectoids and Greys are easily controlled; but not Nordics and humans."

"I'm proud of that and we will employ Winston Churchill tactics and fight in the streets and in alleys and forests until we win. A patriotic President will arise again. All he has to do is promise to make America great again!"

"You just experienced a deep recession and still American jobs were moved to China just when you would expect the opposite. The deck is stacked against you. China will be ruthless when it takes over. God help Japan for what it did at Unit 731 during World War Two. After China there will never be a country like the United States again."

"I'm glad you acknowledged God. The only reason we are building up China is so that they can modernize their military and we can have an enemy so we can maintain our military industrial complex and budget. It's a dangerous strategy. When the word gets out about "Them" we won't need China to hate. What is Unit 731?"

"The Pacific is passive in name only. China has never forgiven Japan for Unit 731 which was a covert chemical and biological research center in China where the Japanese performed horrific experiments on the Chinese during the war after the slaughter of 200,000 Chinese at Nanjing. Japan was just as immoral as the Nazi's."

"Wow that never got the press that Hitler got. You almost make this sound like a race war."

"That's why the races were put here. They observe how you react to differences. America and Brazil are the great racial melting pot experiments."

"Are the races all equal?"

"No, genetically there is as much as a one percent DNA difference between the races if you have the courage to publish the mapping of the human genome. Medically you're all the same."

"One percent doesn't sound like much."

"It is when you consider there is a four percent difference between humans and chimps. Did you know that not all medications work evenly on different racial groups?"

"Yes, are Asians the smartest?"

"No actually Jews are; followed by Asians. Whites, Indians, Eskimo and Hispanics are equal and your African has an IQ lower than the other groups."

"Why if you engineered us?"

"Ever bake a cake? Different ETs engineered different continents. The Nordics engineered Europe. The Greys engineered Asia which accounts for their smaller physical size and facial features. The ones that engineered the Jews told them that they were the chosen people and upped their intelligence a little higher than what is generally agreed upon."

"And what is agreed upon?"

"To not make the creation as smart or strong than the creator. The African engineers were concerned for their physical prowess."

"Again, control. God gave us free will. We will never be controlled for long. How has this turned out elsewhere?"

"Most planets break down into race wars. Very few learn tolerance and integration."

"It just seems like affirmative action is an assault against white and Asian people."

"It is but what's the alternative? Jennifer Lopez, President Obama, Tiger Woods, the tennis Williams sisters, Haley Berry; they were all a plant to create acceptance with a few added modifications. Your entertainment industry will turn all alternative soon to feminize men for the Chinese invasion."

"I thought Serena and Venus Williams were built like men."

"They may have been given a little too much. There was also a plan behind Jackie Robinson and Muhammad Ali; both were meant to change attitudes and paradigms. And when “They” are ready for Asians, “They” will act.”

“I see all races in America uniting against a Chinese enemy. China couldn’t even subdue non-violent Tibet. We would crush them. In 1920 there were less than twenty democratic nations in the world. Today there are nearly 100. I’d say we are winning. We have soft power also like Hollywood, the internet, NASA, tourism and our Universities. Lady you have no idea what you are dealing with. Americans are never stronger than when tested.” I said.

“Then why do you think there is such a strong push to disarm Americans? There are over 400 million guns in America and you are the only country that could defend itself against a Chinese invasion or an ET invasion by a species not much more advanced than yourselves. That’s who is here now; a couple of young ET race’s that are maybe 100 years ahead of you. They are experimenting and learning but there are never more than a few hundred of them at any time. That’s why sightings are not very often and they don’t want to confront your military.”

“When I lived in New York, I didn’t believe in owning a gun but since I moved to Pennsylvania and read the NRA magazine and Constitution, I firmly believe that I will not hand my guns over. Homeland Security will have to pry them from my cold dead hands. My right to self-defense in this violent and controlled world comes before even my right to free speech!"

"John, the future is fluid. If you return to your Constitution and beliefs you can still win this and have a 1000 year reign. A small number of you can even survive the asteroid strike and continue. I'm giving you one scenario if the Dalek race succeeds. When the New Atlantis is built after. . . ."

"Who?"

"Correct, from Doctor Who." Sigrun smiles.

Now I'm confused as to what is true and what is a false flag or disinformation. I didn't think Sigrun had a sense of humor.

"Politics and poetry are lies, but not what I'm telling you." Said Sigrun.

"It sounds like this is too big to ever be disclosed. The Air Force and C.I.A. have it locked down. Do they keep the UFO evidence with Obama's birth certificate and college transcripts?"

"That President said if he had a son he would look like Trayvon Martin. I guess his city would look like your Detroit and his country like Cuba." Said Sigrun.

We both laugh. I'm starting to really like Sigrun.

“One day Cuba will be a Commonwealth of ours. Seriously, did you know that Betty and Barney Hill were Obama’s real parents? Look at when they were abducted and when he was born. Then look at their pictures. That’s why very little is known about him and his upbringing.”

“What?”

Sigrun breaks out laughing.

“I don’t understand how this push for globalization is good for the U.S. We used to produce ninety five percent of everything we used and half of everything in the world but now we outsourced the jobs overseas just when we need the jobs.”

“Think it through. The U.S. is a pawn in this scenario. Economies aren’t controlled by the U.S. or corporations or the Bilderbergers. They let you think there are secret societies of greedy old men but that’s not it. It’s a cover for the social engineering that the ETs do. Everything from the gay and inter-racial relationships in every TV show to the deconstructing of the U.S. from within to the building up of China is controlled by “Them”. America was supposed to be the New Atlantis but it didn’t work out. First “They” tried the League of Nations and then the U.N. and now the Council on Foreign Affairs and the Club of Rome.”

“What good is all this technology if most people just go home and watch an electronic reproduction of life? Most people miss out on living life.” I said.

“Owners and CEOs should earn twenty five times what a worker earns. That’s the universal norm. When the top earns 500 times what the worker earns like they do now, you fall into decadence where the top one percent can focus on luxury, sex and huge entertainment and sporting events while the bottom has to choose between welfare and minimum wage.”

“You’ve opened my eyes. When Corporations go global they no longer care about America, just where they can earn the highest profit. That’s why good jobs are moved and the replacement jobs are minimum wage. I bet the top earners will earn 1000 to one soon.”

“Your internet will create a revolution like the printing press did. When people can instantly access information, they become dangerous to the powers to be. “They” observe whether restrictions are put on the internet or does freedom prevail. That’s why they pulled away from you. America keeps failing its Founding Aliens, I mean Fathers.”

“What I see missing is Nationalism. Pride in America.”

"That's part of the experiment. Do the people wake up or look the other way because they are given what they need. Nationalism goes against Globalization."

Changing the subject, I ask, "Is Heidi Klum and Kim Kardashian ETs?"

"Yes hybrids."

"On other planets, is there a one world government or different countries?"

"On most, the entire planet is governed by a one world government." Said Sigrun

"So let me get this right. They want to inter-marry the races so we all look Brazilian. They want us all to have one vote. They want to redistribute the jobs and wealth to all people and disarm us. Is that correct?"

"Correct, the world is just a business. The world government plan is well advanced. The destruction of America's dominance is what delays it. It will involve moving economies away from the dollar and martial law and a culling of Patriots by enlisted Patriots in order to implement it." Said Sigrun.

"The very people who are loyal to America need to be eliminated?"

"Yes, America became too dominant and needs to be destroyed from within with liberal disinformation programs. What good is a world of eight billion people that are dominated by less than five percent of the population? America follows the same corporate model where Americans earn 500 times what the third world-earns."

"You mean by Europeans and Americans. Maybe we are just the most capable group on the planet. There are five billion Chinese, Muslims and Indians. There are 320 million Americans. Maybe Europe and North America should form a Western Culture Union and become one mega country to combat China or the ETs? We can call it Western Union. Kind of has a familiar ring to it. That would give us almost one billion educated people and most of the world's economy. This won't end well for us if we are brought down to the same level as the rest of the people on earth. Why would I want to give an equal vote to these other groups with my money?"

"You need to think as a species, not an individual."

"Just like a hive mentality. You never did believe in freedom because we won out and you can't control us. God forbid if all eight billion of us were free and uncontrollable! You need to dumb us down with socialism."

"Correct, ultimately it's all about control." Said Sigrun with a big smile on her face.

"You mentioned secret societies, but there have always been secret societies since the time of Egypt. I've read about them and they are always featured on the History Channel."

"Yes, some Atlantian's escaped the destruction and fled to Egypt. They were the master builders who later became the Free Masons and Templars. These were never the major players. The Gnostics were anti-women and anti-Catholic. The Rosicrucian's delved into the occult in order to find secret knowledge from the other side."

"Rosicrucian means rose and cross." I said.

"Correct, the Catholic Church inadvertently forced the creation of these societies by their suppression of free thought and they forced science underground with their persecution of Bruno, Copernicus and Galileo. These societies were a reaction to the church, nothing more."

"So the Bush family isn't behind this with their Skull and Bones Society?"

"Listen very carefully. "They" are behind the new world order. They want one government, one economy, one military, one society and one Muslim religion because it is less free and very controlled with Sharia law. It only takes one world crisis to accept the new world order. Remember what I said about controlling the media."

“Islam is a Christian heresy. President Kennedy was right when he said that secrecy is repugnant in a free society and there is a conspiracy to subvert, intimidate and infiltrate the government. Dissenters are silenced instead of praised.”

“Like Julian Assange and Eric Snowden.” Said Sigrun with a smile.

After a pause I ask. “Did the Vikings and Templars come to America before Columbus?”

“Many groups did and yes they both did. The Templars came here in 1307 after the Pope and King of France seized their land and assets. They hide the Arc of the Covenant in Nova Scotia and some came to America. Your Francis Bacon probably had as large an impact on your history as Ben Franklin did.”

“What did he ever do?”

“He was the real Shakespeare and a hybrid. Bacon was a Rosicrucian who printed thousands of underground free books and stood up to the church but used aliases in his literary works. That is why you rarely hear of him. Bacon was an admirer of Athena, The Greek ET Goddess, who would shake her spear at the eyes of ignorance. Hence you get Shakespeare. Bacons group wrote all the plays attributed to William. That’s why there are different styles in his plays as if a painting was completed by multiple artists.”

"I guess there are more things in Heaven and Earth than we've ever dreamed of. So if it is not about oil and gold then why do we deny the ET existence?" I ask.

"It is all about getting the technology for the Americans and Brits. That's why they assign UFOs to their Department of Defense when other countries assign it to their F.A.A. as an air safety issue."

I ask, "Did they create the flux capacitor?"

"The what?"

She had no idea what I was talking about and apparently never saw the movie *Back to the Future*. "Has anyone tried to get the truth out?"

"Yes, three times. Forrestal in "49"; the "64" meeting with Eisenhower and in "97" with Governor Fife Symington."

"I know of the Eisenhower meeting at Muroc and Symington making fun of the issue at a press conference but what's the truth with Forrestal?"

"Symington had a chance to blow this wide open and he passed because he was in legal trouble and they pressured him to debunk the Phoenix lights. Forrestal was another story. He was your first Secretary of Defense and in "47" he met the captured Roswell ET. That creature made telepathic contact with Forrestal and showed him the truth in hopes of gaining his freedom from the underground cell. They hate to be kept underground; it's a form of torture for "Them". Forrestal was against keeping the ET issue above top secret and said at a Staff meeting in 1949 that he was going to the press. Fife Symington's older cousin, Secretary of the Air Force Stuart Symington, met with Forrestal and escorted him to Bethesda Naval Hospital where he was confined for a mental breakdown. He was confined even though two months earlier he was awarded the Distinguished Service Medal by President Truman. He was confined to the sixteenth floor even though the hospital staff recommended a ground floor room for a man in his supposed mental state. Your C.I.A. controlled LBJ was the last person to speak with him. They couldn't change Forrestal's mind so when his brother threatened to check him out, they staged a suicide and threw him out the sixteenth floor window. Forrestal fought back and the window sill had numerous scuff marks on it but a tight noose around his neck tied loosely to a radiator ended his life. Fife had knowledge of his distant cousin's involvement with Forrestal fifty years earlier and elected not to go public in "97" out of fear for his life and prosecution. He was wrong!"

"It's such a shame that no one has the fortitude to stand up. I used to think that Obama was a left wing liberal Manchurian candidate that might disclose the truth but he turned out to be a "good" American President. He violated the Constitution more than President Bush and spied on Americans and killed more people with drone strikes than his predecessor. He got forty percent of the population dependent on government handouts. How does a guy like him do a complete about face from his campaign promises?" I ask.

"The N.S.A. had the goods on Obama and he had to cooperate or his legacy would be destroyed with an impeachment. But to coin a phrase; UFOs are above top secret and Obama was a hybrid inserted as President to Socialize America. Many people have been killed to keep the ET truth quiet. We've already discussed the sixty two scientists working on Hitler's Bell project along with; Forrestal's suicide, Ruppelt's heart attack and Phil Schneider's cancer-suicide. There was also James MacDonald's suicide, Hynek's cancer; John Mack was hit by a car, Karla Turner's cancer, William Cooper was gunned down, Morris Jessup's suicide, Congressman Schiff's cancer, Budd Hopkins cancer, Phillip Coppens cancer and not to mention Lincoln and Kennedy. That idiot Hinckley was supposed to kill Reagan but missed. It only delayed the inevitable decline of America."

"How about UFO radio host Kevin Smith? I did my first radio interview with him in 2008 and was on his show seven times."

"Yes, he had two million listeners and was becoming dangerous."

“The reporter who covered the Kecksburg story also got hit by a car; John Murphy. There were also twenty two British aerospace engineers and scientists working on Star Wars that all committed suicide in the “80’s”. I also read an article that there have been 137 Ufologists who died suspiciously over the last twenty years. It seems like the lifespan of a serious Ufologist falls far short of the national average.” I added.

“Frank Edwards and three other Ufologists died on the morning of June 24, 1967 before the start of the *World UFO Conference* hosted by Gray Barker in New York City. Edwards was the original Art Bell on radio and was only 58, like you. Others that were killed were Frank Scully, Ivan Sanderson and Stanley Kubrick after faking the Apollo landing. Eleven microbiologists working on alien viruses died in a four month period in 2002 after the virus was obtained.”

“There were also two MUFON investigators that died suddenly; Ron Johnson and Ann Livingston. My question is whether these people died from the psychological stress implied by the subject of superior ET beings controlling and manipulating us or did an agency kill them or was it premature deaths as reported?”

“All of the above. But more importantly, disclosure will come from your Pope. It is already planned. Why do you think the Vatican has an advanced telescope and observatory in Rome and Arizona of all places? Three times they have made statements that there is life in space and that they are our brothers. The Pope is the only one that could let the U.S. government off the hook. Your President will say he had no prior proof and the Pope will say it is the *First Contact*. He'll put a religious spin on it and everyone wins except for the Ufologists."

"Power corrupts and ultimate power corrupts ultimately. I have an idea and would like your opinion. You opened my eyes regarding taking freedom for granted. What if someone created encryption software for every email, Facebook post and internet order. What if someone created anonymity of the internet?"

"The person who creates that software or replaces steel with graphene will be the next billionaire!"

"Are there any earthlike worlds where they look like us?"

"Yes, many. There are the ones that interceded in your evolution as your missing link and others."

"Tell me about one such species."

"There is an earth in another dimension. The inhabitants look similar to you except they are a foot shorter and have no hair. They are a female dominated species where the males are used as laborers and for reproduction. They are allowed three partners starting at age twenty each for twenty years. Their first two partners pair forty year olds with twenty year olds for training and reproduction. Their last partner at sixty is the same age until they expire. There is no divorce but if they abuse a spouse, they lose privileges until the next mating age comes about. The females are nearly twice as intelligent and very aggressive like your female lions. The females also retain the memories of their past three generations and speak as though they have lived those prior two lives."

"So what's different? Sounds like earth."

"They had an encounter with Maria Christo who they thought was the return of their savior only she was the anti-Christo. A great war ensued that nearly destroyed the planet. Your anti-Christ was born recently and walks the earth."

"It feels like we are close to the end time when right is wrong and good is evil. Where do all the missing people go?"

No answer.

"Do "They" have zoo's?"

"Don't ask me that."

"Are humans in their zoo's?"

"Are reptiles in yours?"

"Do "They" have wax museums with replicas from around the universe?"

"Yes and originals in "Their" museums."

"I'd very much like to see one. Maybe one day we'll have a UFO truth museum at the national Mall in D.C."

"Whatever you do, avoid contact and capture. They don't have your best interests at heart."

"Where else does the missing go?"

"Prey to be hunted as game, eaten, sacrificed to appease, gladiators in an arena, museums, zoos and genetic experiments."

"I'm trying to understand all that you have said. There are beings from other planets, other dimensions, the Hollow Earth, Angels and Demons; some are good and some are bad just like us; and most are trying to teach us or use us as an experiment. What about time travel? Don't we ever come back to alter the past?"

"We call it time-share. Yes you do and can but you don't change what already happened and there is no way of going forward in time. It is a one way trip. The events that occurred and the lives that lived stay the same. It's like taking a plane flight from New York to Los Angeles. You pick up three hours in time but it doesn't mean the three hours didn't occur. If you went back and killed Hitler or stepped on a butterfly during the prehistoric times, nothing will change in your dimension. It immediately does start a new dimension and parallel world right next to the other. All the people duplicate and have different memories and experiences from that point forward. The two never merge. The people who came back in time don't disappear. It is not a domino effect. You just create different dimensions."

"Hmmm, not sure that makes sense. Have we tried it yet or is time travel something we will do someday?"

"You tried it with that botched Philadelphia experiment. Crew members got lodged into walls and floors. What a disaster. But you learned from it."

"I would like to go back and meet Jesus."

"If you did, you cannot look upon his face. You would immediately go blind. It happened twice already and no further efforts to contact him are permitted."

"I'm surprised they didn't go back in time with different Dead Sea scrolls that dispute Jesus."

"They did but nothing changed. Jesus is too powerful."

I think to myself because he is the son of God and all that she has told me is a demonic deception. God created us and there is no evolution and therefore no life in space. "By the way, what is your last name?" I asked.

"Eve, and on that note you can drop me off on the corner of the I-25 intersection."

"But you are still seven or eight miles from Santa Fe."

"That's ok, I'm meeting someone else."

Before she got out she posed a rhetorical question.

"There is another event horizon coming. Not just the asteroid. When "They" come again for a mass harvesting, they will go to the southern hemisphere or third world countries. Why would they confront the U.S. or Russia or China or Europe where there could be heavy casualties on both sides? It's always been easier in Africa, the Middle East, Southeast Asia and South America. That's the art of war. You will soon be able to genetically engineer humans that can stand up to them. Rather than waiting for a million year evolutionary change, you will create one like we, I mean they, created you. Then there will be an agreement or war. It's the way it has been on all habitable planets. So when they arrive like Independence Day and disclosure is indisputable, but they are only hovering over third world countries, how will you react? Will you secure your borders and coasts and station your subs and aircraft carriers and military off the east and west coasts of the U.S. or will you weaken your defenses and go to the aid of Africa and Asia and South America? That's how it will be. How it's always been; part of the test. How will you react? Protect the world or protect your borders?"

I replied, "We will protect OUR borders as it should be. Maybe we should offer them the most unproductive low IQ people who are on social services and solve all of our financial problems? Do you know what Eschatology is?"

"No."

"It's when man does something so horrible or creates such an unfixable situation that we force the return of Jesus to save us. That's what we are talking about."

"So after all I've told you, you think this is about the *Rapture*? That should've happened after what Hitler did."

Sigrun just shakes her head and says, "Do what thou wilt", another Free Mason term.

"So how do we get the truth out, the proof?"

"The truth is out there. You have to follow the trail."

"What trail?"

"There is a hidden trail that leads to the UFO proof. You start at Baalbek Lebanon and you will find a Freemason symbol only the G in the center of the symbol doesn't stand for geometry. It stands for Gobekli-tepe Turkey. If you go to Gobekli-tepe you will find a star map that leads you to the Sphinx in Egypt. On the left paw there is a Mayan symbol that leads you to Tikal Peru and the Popol Vuh sacred document. The Popol Vuh has a symbol for Stonehenge. In England you will find a crop circle painting which is really a musical note that leads you to the Palazzo Vecchio in Florence Italy and the Madonna painting. Behind the painting you will find a page from Columbus's journal that leads you to the Vatican. Remember, the painting was made in 1449 and the journal page is from 1492. At the Vatican, which is the oldest running institution on earth, you will find the Papal Prophecy that mentions Roswell on page 47 as a cryptogram. In Roswell, you will find a copy of the 1686 Plurality of Worlds which has the "E Pluribus Unum" and eye above the pyramid symbol from the U.S. dollar bill. The eye and top of the pyramid stands for the obelisk at the Washington monument in your nation's capital. If you look at the measurements of the monument, it is 6666 inches high and 666 inches wide. If you add those numbers together you get 6 and 9. The 69 symbol is reversible and stands for the Freemasons term, "As above, so below". Buried below the Washington Monument is a real time capsule from my people that explains the true history I just told you".

"Forget about the *da Vinci Code* or *National Treasure*. This is a quest in the making and I think I will eventually end up on the religious path!"

I let her off at the intersection and look at the clock on the car dash and it is 6:47 pm. How did it take almost eight hours to drive 178 miles with a quick lunch stop? I proceed to the Hilton hotel where I record everything she had told me. I realize that she gave me the String Theory of everything. Right before I arrive at my hotel, I round a corner and the sun strikes one of those crosses that family members put up at the site of a fatal car crash on the side of the road. It must've been made of metal since it shown brightly and momentarily blinded me and I could feel the warmth of the cross on my face. I couldn't help but wonder if that wasn't a sign or reminder that one's faith in God will be tested.

I believe in that simple man who had no formal education, never wrote a word and never owned a home or had a family or visited a major city yet in just three years became the most important figure in human history. Oh how I would've preferred a close encounter with Jesus than this alien hybrid demon. This encounter greatly reinforced my faith. I have suspected for some time now that some alien encounters are demonic infestations but I also wonder, are angels misidentified ETs or are ETs misidentified angels? But more importantly, what if God was wrong about us? What if while "His" spirit is in us, we can tap into some of "His" latent abilities and become God-like? I have no proof of this encounter and I ask none to believe me.

All there ever was or will be are angels and shape shifting fallen angels in reference to the unexplained world of the paranormal....

THE MUFON FILES (PT. 1)
?
AN INTERVIEW WITH JOHN VENTRE
Photo: Los Angeles Times, February 25, 1942 - "The Battle of Los Angeles"

Atheists tend to have a higher rate of suicide.

Atheists Jackson Pollack committed suicide and Nietzsche went mad because there was no hope.

Evolution dictates that all are not meant to survive.

When you use Gods name in vain, you are still acknowledging his supreme power……

When a child is born, it clinches its hand to grab onto anything and everything. When a senior dies, his hands are open because he can't take anything with him….

Chapter Three

THE CASE FOR UFOs

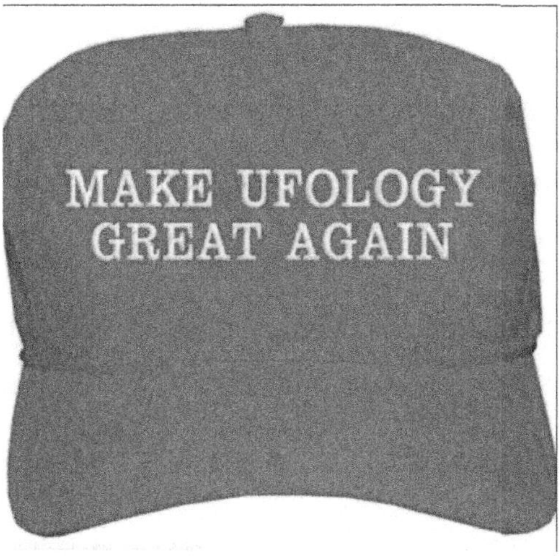

"Google Before You Giggle"

Since becoming Pennsylvania, Delaware, Vermont, Rhode Island, Maine, Massachusetts, West Virginia and New Hampshire State Director for the Mutual UFO Network in 2007, I decided that I had better do some research and become a subject matter expert on UFOs. What I found astounded me. The history of UFOs over earth goes back centuries. It can be traced through every culture and every time period of our so called "evolution". I had heard of rock carvings, Nazca lines and ancient tales. Interestingly, these ancient cultures all speak of acquiring knowledge from star people and Gods. The miracles performed in the time of Moses lead the Egyptians to try and invent the failed science of alchemy. Most cultures also de-evolved into ritual human sacrifices to these Gods. Will history repeat itself? The true recorded history of ancient man was destroyed in 391 AD when the Romans destroyed the library of Alexandria in Egypt. A second repository may lie under the left paw of the sphinx in Egypt. Then again, maybe the descendants of Adam were smarter with pure DNA and latent abilities and did build all these structures and we have it in reverse.....

(Courtesy Sandeep Karunakaran-India)

The more you investigate this field, the more you learn and cannot dismiss the inconvenient facts. What surprised me were the Renaissance paintings and biblical connection to UFOs along with the many government documents and the covert interference regarding UFO research. Why did the C.I.A. create a situation where reputable scientists will not investigate this enigma? Was it deliberate or an accident of the cover-up? Now, we will never know our true history.

Sumerian is our oldest text and Hindu is the oldest religion we know of. Both date back to 6000 BC. The Hindu Mahabharata was written 3500 years ago after being passed down through word of mouth and speaks of flying craft with detailed flight manuals and a detailed nuclear battle in Mohenjo-Daro India (now Pakistan). Skeletons found there are 50 times more radioactive than they should be and sand and rock have been vitrified from high heat. You should read some of the excerpts from it or watch my lecture, "*UFOs in Art and History*" on my website.

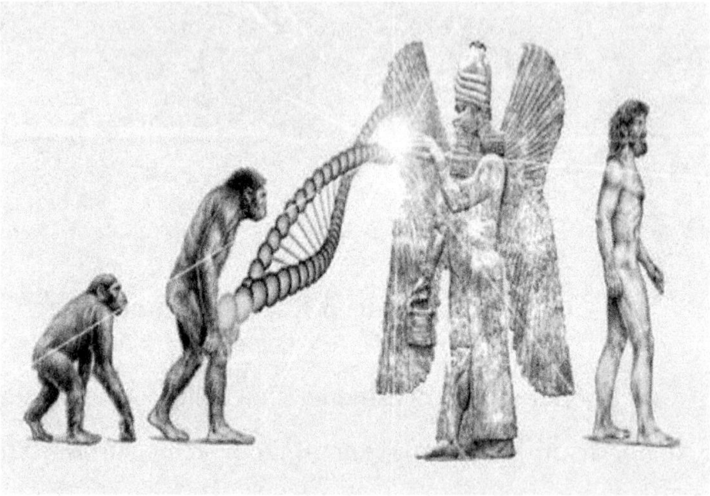

In Abydos Egypt, there is a 4600 year old structure that contains a plaque with five modern aircraft and subs depicted. You also have to ask why the older pyramids were nearly perfectly built and in alignment with the compass while the newer imitations were poorly built and are crumbling. In Baalbek Lebanon there are 1200 ton stones that were quarried 50 miles away. Who lifted them? These ancient structures were surely built with advanced technology by non-humans or by the Nephilim who were upgraded hybrid humans. Ancient aliens or ancient deities? Our modern cranes cannot lift these huge stones.

I give many examples of UFO/ET involvement and interference in our history from Egypt to all wars to the present. But what is their origin and agenda?

The Mayans and other South American cultures had the legend of the Viracochas who were a tall white race with elongated skulls that came from the sky and would return again. Kukulcan was said to have come from the stars.

The Black Plague originated in China in 1333 and spread to Europe in 1347. Although it is blamed on fleas and rats, there are more accounts that describe lights in the sky and a foul mist that followed suggesting that a UFO sprayed an infectious biological agent to eradicate earth of humans. For all the "new agers" who believe "They" are here to help, give me one solid example!

At the Palazzo Vecchio in Florence Italy, there hangs a 600 year old painting of the Madonna and Saint Giovanni. In the lower right hand corner, there is a man and his dog looking up at a UFO. In the upper left hand corner, there is a mother ship with many smaller craft emerging and a man and his dog looking up at them. Painters in this time period painted what they actually saw, not abstract painting.

On January 24, 1878, John Martin of Dallas Texas saw a strange dark object in the sky that he described as a saucer to the Dennison Daily News who wrote an article entitled, "A Strange Phenomenon". It was actually Martin and not Kenneth Arnold that coined the flying saucer term.

Prior to 1800, there are only around 60 quality UFO reports on record. There are another 200 in the 1800's and another 100 from 1900-1940. A strange increase in UFO cases started with World War Two, almost in tandem with Adolph Hitler. One has to wonder if there wasn't an unholy alliance. Could the same force be behind Herod's first male born infanticide and Hitler's holocaust and todays abductions? The human experiments by the Nazi's on the Jews and the Japanese on the Chinese mirror the human abduction phenomena of today.

(Courtesy Banksy Bristol)

In the 1940's and 1950's, most UFO news was given to the press from our Air Force. Examples are the Battle of LA in 1942, Roswell in 1947 and the UFOs over our Capital in 1952. There was a UFO Officer assigned to all military bases and the position is mentioned in many documents from that time period. In 1948, Project Sign was formed to get an estimate of the situation and concluded UFOs were real and extraterrestrial. Project Grudge followed in 1951 when the Air Force asked that the Navy study UFOs but were forced to accept the assignment. In 1952, the name was changed to Project Blue Book. The C.I.A. got involved in 1953 with the Robertson Panel and their conclusion was to discredit, debunk and infiltrate UFO groups.

In 1954, the airlines industry and the Pentagon agreed to impose military restrictions on commercial pilots that reported UFOs to the media. Pilots would be subject to espionage laws and a $10,000 fine and ten years in prison.

In 1960, The Brookings Institute in Washington, DC conducted a study entitled "Proposed Studies on the Implications of Peaceful Space Activities" with a section entitled "Implications of Extraterrestrial life". Their conclusion was that there would be profound social consequences and that society could break down. Religious, Scientific and Engineering groups would be devastated by the discovery of superior beings. These findings were presented before the 82nd Congress on April 18, 1961. I would like to comment that they do have superior technology but if they are abducting humans, then they are not morally superior to us! Vice Admiral Hillenkoetter, who was our first C.I.A. Director, called for continued Congressional hearings on UFOs and became a Board member of NICAP.

In 1962, General MacArthur addressed the West Point Military Academy by saying, "One day we may be faced with an ultimate conflict between a united human race and the sinister forces of some other planetary galaxy".

Shortly after Gemini 7 astronauts Frank Borman and James Lovell reported saying and seeing "a bogey, we have several sightings" on December 9, 1965, an acorn shaped object landed in Kecksburg, Pa. The object made a southeast turn near Cleveland and made a controlled minimal crash landing just east of Pittsburgh with minimal impact. Witnesses saw symbols or Cyrillic writing on its base. The U.S. Army showed up in force warning residents that they have orders to shoot to kill and flat bedded an object out of the woods. The military claims they only sent three officers to the scene. A local radio reporter, John Murphy, was told he couldn't air the story he wrote. Murphy died in a hit and run car accident a few years later. In 2015, Owen Eichler and I identified a GE Mark 2 spy satellite that came down that day that was able to maneuver. A soviet space probe, Cosmos 96, came down 13 hours earlier. A GE Mark 2 spy capsule from Johnson Island near Hawaii lost its orbit 39 hours earlier and no one knows where it landed. The shape of the crashed object matched the Nazi Bell program.

The Sci-Fi channel sued NASA for the Kecksburg records and won in court. A NASA spokesperson said they examined fragments from Kecksburg which were from a soviet object but NASA claimed the box of records were lost. One of my investigators, Ed Woomer, believes the symbols are motion hieroglyphics that when spun look like something else or can generate power. In 2016, Owen and I located the Army Colonel that headed up the Kecksburg retrieval. This proves Project Bluebook lied. Read our research paper in my book *Case for UFOs*. How many of these crashes are really military experimental craft and not ET?

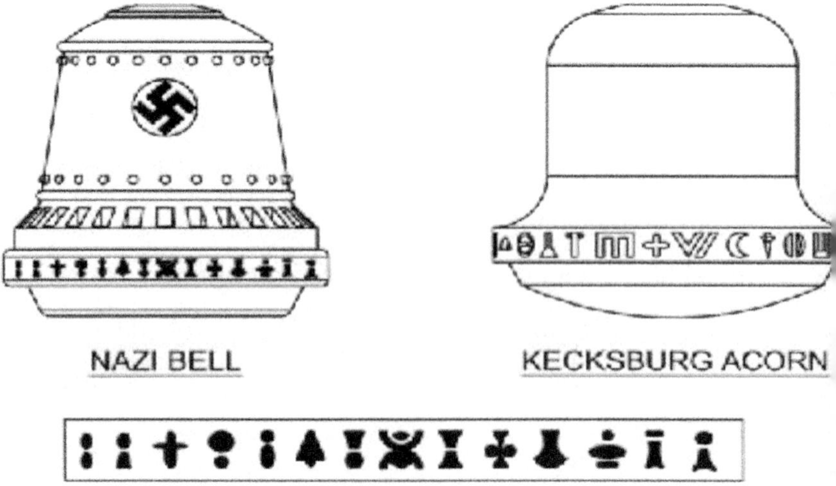

NOTE: STRANGE INSCRIPTIONS WERE FOUND ON BOTH THE NAZI BELL AND KECKSBURG ACORN

THEY DROVE IT, OUT OF THE WOODS.
AND IVE SEEN MANY ARMY TRUCKS
THIS ONE HAD A WHITE STAR ON THE
SIDES. I REMEMBER VERY CLEARLY.

I WOULD SWEAR ON THE BIBLE AND
TAKE A LIE DETECTOR TEST.

YOURS TRULY
MR. JERRY BETTERS
Jerry Betters
5330 FERN St. #405
Pgh. PA. 15224

Kevin D. Buckner
Notarial Seal
Kevin D. Buckner, Notary Public
Pittsburgh, Allegheny County
My Commission Expires Mar. 7, 2005
Member, Pennsylvania Association of Notaries

Attachment 13

(Courtesy Huffington Post)

The lost GE Mark 2 RV from Dec 7 looks just like witness Jerry Betters notarized drawing above.

In October 1966, a UFO was tracked on radar outside of Minot AFB in North Dakota. It activated the missile silo alarms and the 20 ton missile silo door was found opened. Also in 1966, Congressman Gerald Ford asked for and got Congressional hearings on UFOs due to the complaints by Michigan residents.

In March 1967, a UFO shut down 10 missiles at the Echo Flight facility in Montana and a week later did the same at Malmstrom AFB in Montana. Twenty Minute Man missiles were deactivated. Also in 1967, Senator Barry Goldwater requested access to the Blue Room at Wright Patterson AFB. General Curtis LeMay flatly denied him access but did mention a UFO file and above top-secret storage area. Senator Goldwater became a Board member of NICAP.

In 1968, Senator Robert Kennedy stated that he was a card-carrying member of the Amalgamated Flying Saucer Assoc. and expressed his interest in the subject in at least two letters. Also in 1968, an internal Rand document written by George Kocher (UFOs: What to Do? Nov 27 1968 doc # 18154-PR) noted that there would be worldwide panic and that based on the C.I.A. funded Robertson Panel's recommendation, the Government must "deny and ridicule" UFOs and discourage citizens from taking any active interest in the subject. On July 29, 1968, Illinois Senator

Donald Rumsfeld attended a Symposium on UFOs before the 19th Congress House of Representatives. This is the same Donald Rumsfeld who recently said that $2.3 trillion, which was revised down to $300 Billion, has disappeared into black projects. I would challenge you to find Congressional hearings on Bigfoot, ghosts, fairies, elves or other topics of so called "make believe". Walter Cronkite hosted a CBS TV special organized by the C.I.A. to debunk UFOs. That's what the public remembers since they seem to believe everything they see on TV. The University of Colorado received $523K in funding to study UFOs and put Dr. Condon in charge. Dr. Condon quickly stated that UFOs were nonsense and an internal memo was leaked where a strategy to trick the public was discussed.

On July 16, 1969, a United States law was passed entitled, "Extra-Terrestrial Exposure Law" (Title 14, Section 1211 of the Code of Federal Regulations). It makes it illegal for the public to come into contact with extra-terrestrials or their vehicles. An individual can be fined up to $5000 and imprisoned for up to one year and be quarantined by NASA without a hearing. In 1991, the law was rescinded after the realization that if someone was prosecuted, it would be confirmation!

From 1968 through 1970, the Air Force Academy in Colorado Springs taught a Physics 370 class to Cadets where Chapter 33 was entitled "Unidentified Flying Objects". The class discusses the 47,000-year history of UFOs along with prominent cases and comments that, "The phenomenon deserves valid scientific study". Their conclusion was that, "many witnesses have been reliable people and it is doubtful that the phenomenon was entirely psychological. This leaves us with the unpleasant possibility of alien visitors. Data suggests that there are three and maybe four different groups of aliens. It is best to keep an open mind and not take a position on either side of the question". The Physics course was edited and revised in early 1970 and eventually removed in 1971.

MUFON was founded in 1969 after the U.S. Air Force concluded seventeen years of UFO investigations through Project Blue Book. Their conclusion was that UFOs pose no threat to our National Security. Government UFO investigations officially ended and the Physics 370 class were cancelled at the Air Force Academy after 1970. An October 1969 letter from Air Force Brigadier General Bolender stated that UFO investigations that posed a threat to National Security would continue to be investigated by the Air Force and were not part of Project Blue Book. These UFO investigations, as in the past, would be handled in accordance with directive JANAP 146 and Air Force Manual 55-11. MUFON is a private citizen voluntary investigative organization. Dr. James McDonald and the American Institute of Aeronautics both recommended the continued study of UFOs.

The Project Blue Book years were marked by the most fascinating spy drama that pitted the C.I.A. sponsored Blue Book and Dr Condon along with J. Allen Hynek against the public and NICAP led by Major Donald Keyhoe, Admiral Hillenkoetter, Captain Ruppelt and later Dr James MacDonald and Leonard Stringfield. NICAP's efforts to get Congressional hearings were constantly thwarted by the secretive C.I.A. and eventually led to the resignation of Ruppelt and Hillenkoetter from NICAP on the eve of possible Congressional hearings and the eventual infiltration of NICAP by C.I.A. agents and NICAP's demise. Even APRO, a Midwest UFO organization, was under surveillance and infiltration by the C.I.A. and they also closed up shop. MUFON is the last group standing.

On January 27, 1976, Washington, London and Moscow signed the Treaty on Exploration and use of Outer Space. A total of 115 countries have since signed this treaty. It basically says that nuclear weapons cannot be put in space and that all discoveries from space must be shared. Here lies the problem with the back engineering of the Roswell craft.

"In 1987, attitudes began to change. Claims centered on a long term relationship between "Them" and us. They were here to stay; a deal was struck. Abductions were taking place on a scale never before contemplated in exchange for technology. Humanity was sold out pawns used by aliens for genetic material. They were creating human-alien hybrids. Missing children were actually being consumed" (Richard Dolan, "UFOs and the National Security State").

In 1992, William Kramer and Charles Bahme copyrighted the "Fire Officers Guide to Disaster Control" which is used in every Fire Dept. in the U.S. This book is a national guide and FEMA approved. Chapter Thirteen discusses "Enemy Attack and UFO Potential. In this chapter we will turn our attention to the very real threat posed by UFOs". The Chapter mirrors the Air Force Cadet class while discussing the 50,000 year history of UFOs, classification systems, recent cases and of course a warning. While citing the Federal Law (previously mentioned), "Near approaches of UFOs can be harmful to humans". Charles Bahme was also a witness to the Feb 1942 "Battle of LA" as a teenager.

In 1995, the Clinton's met with Laurance Rockefeller at his ranch in Wyoming and discussed UFOs. Here you can see Hillary carrying Paul Davies book, "Are we Alone".

Above is a picture of Hillary Clinton with Rockefeller at his ranch in Wyoming in 1995:

In 1999, France's COMETA association (committee for in depth studies; their civilian version of NASA) published "UFOs and Defense". The report highlights recent cases, hypotheses, implications, UFOs and defense and a conclusion that, "The U.S. holds a position of military superiority over other countries. It is impossible for them to divulge the sources of this research".

We have the technology and are not willing to share even though we signed the Outer Space Treaty. I'm glad that the U.S. has this technology and Iran, China or North Korea doesn't. I'm certain, in a perverted way, that the CIA and Pentagon are actually protecting us from the UFO truth.

President Reagan referenced an armed conflict with extraterrestrials in five separate United Nations speeches because he saw a UFO on two occasions.

In 2002, a Roper poll was conducted. Three out of four claimed that they were psychologically prepared for Government Disclosure and that 88% said it would not affect their religious beliefs. More than half, 56%, believed UFOs were real and 48% believed that we have been visited. Two thirds believed that there is intelligent life in our universe and 45% believed that we were being monitored; and 21% believed in abductions. A 2008 AOL

News poll of 138,507 adults indicated that 93% believed in life elsewhere and 81% believed that earth had been visited.

In 2007, New Mexico Governor Bill Richardson asked for Congressional hearings on what really happened in Roswell. At the 2007 Democrat Presidential candidate's debate, Ohio Rep Dennis Kucinich stated that he had seen a UFO while at Shirley MacLaine's home. Former Arizona Governor Fife Symington also came clean that he saw a UFO in 1997 during the Phoenix Lights incident. Astronauts Buzz Aldrin and Gordon Cooper claim to have seen UFOs. Edgar Mitchell has stated on numerous occasions that he has been privy to information that UFOs and other life forms do exist.

In the past decade, a group of distinguished witnesses gathered four times at the National Press Club in Washington DC and signed affidavits that they were willing to testify before Congress. In 2001 Dr. Steven Greer organized 21 military, government and scientific witnesses that told their story. He also identified 350 additional witnesses that were willing to come forward. Their affidavit requested a Congressional inquiry and to utilize this new energy source for good and to stop the weaponization of space.

In 2007 Investigative Journalist Leslie Kean and Producer James Fox organized 19 witnesses; 13 pilots, 5 foreign Generals and former Arizona Governor Fife Symington who testified to what they saw regarding UFOs.

In 2010 Robert Hastings organized seven U.S. Military officers and one enlisted man to testify at the National Press club that UFOs have violated our nuclear facilities. They also produced 120 additional signatures from witnesses on an affidavit that is being ignored by Congress. The Air Force response was that "There have been NO significant cases to warrant an investigation since the conclusion of Project Blue Book in 1969". Somehow they missed our Minuteman missiles being turned off at Malmstrom AFB in 1967 and 2007 even though they do not have a turn off switch. They also missed the same at Nellis AFB in 2003 in the presence of a UFO. Since Project Blue Book ended we have had Bentwaters, the Phoenix Lights, O'Hare airport, Stephenville, the Pennsylvania UFO wave in 2008 and a host of other sightings. CNN and the Tribune Review covered the National Press club story in a positive light. The Washington Post debunked and mocked the officers.

In 2013, The Citizen's Hearing was facilitated by five former Congress people; Lynn Wooley, Carolyn Kilpatrick, Merrill Cook, Darlene Hooley, Roscoe Bartlett along with Senator Mike Gravel and Attorney Daniel Sheehan. Steven Bassett organized the hearings. The setting was a Congressional Hearing where testimony was given and thirty eight witnesses were questioned by the panel. Topics covered included UFO history, the

Rockefeller Initiative, RAF Bentwaters, Nuclear bases, documents, Roswell, International cases, pilots and technology.

In 2014, "*Hangar 1: The UFO Files*" TV show debuted on H2 and moved to the larger History Channel in 2015 and tripled its viewership. It took 45 years to get the files of the Mutual UFO Network on TV to inform the public. The show was abruptly cancelled after 20 successful episodes. When you lay out the timeline of documents from the 1940's through present day, no intelligent human being can believe that the UFO phenomenon is not real. But where do they originate from and for what purpose?

Did you know that on three separate occasions in 1957 by Father Connell, 2001 by Father Balducci and 2008 by Father Funes, the Vatican made a statement regarding the possibility of extraterrestrial life in space? "God in all his eminence and power has also created life in space. It would be arrogant of us to believe that we are the only intelligent species in the universe. They are our Brothers and have fallen from grace just as we have". The Vatican leases time from NASA on the LUCIFER advanced infrared telescope in Tucson and is prepared for contact and disclosure will come from the Vatican and not from any government or individual. I'll explain more as you read on.

When it comes to eyewitness testimony, experts say that it is unreliable. Seems odd that three people can see a man steal a woman's purse, call the police, testify in court, have twelve jurors convict even though the purse was never recovered and the three witnesses and twelve jurors can leave the courtroom, look up and see a UFO and not be believed. Eyewitness testimony is the basis for our criminal justice system. I hope we are prepared to free twenty percent of our prisoners if eyewitness testimony is unreliable!

When I'm asked, "Why don't extraterrestrials make contact with us", I can't help but wonder if they are observing us and they see we can't accept each other because we are white, brown, black and yellow. Then how could we accept them if they are green or gray? When we accept ourselves as one human race, then maybe they will make contact. But who are "They"? There is more to this phenomenon than meets the eye. Why can't "They" accomplish their goal in thousands of years? Realistically, how much alien abduction does it take to get enough DNA? Why do craft just disappear? You can't ignore the Bible and fallen angels either. Are we experiencing demons in shape shifting alien clothing preparing us for the great deception? Are we being deceived, misdirected or taken over?

With all of that said if it is more comfortable to be a skeptic, at least be an informed skeptic!

Don't you wish whoever builds those gigantic perfectly geometric crop circles overnight would fix our roads?

2017 Interview

My first TV interview in 2008

Wouldn't "They" have just collected DNA?

Courtesy Getty Images

Do not be afraid, for I am with you.

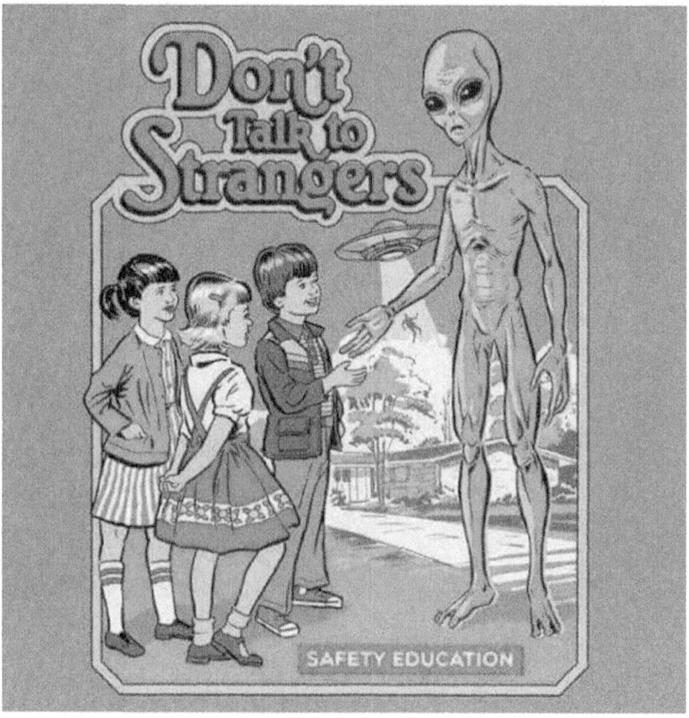
Don't Talk to Strangers
SAFETY EDUCATION

Chapter Four

Trans-Humanism

Mankind and Intelligent Life of Tomorrow

By Micah Hanks

At some point in the lineage of humankind's time here on Earth, our early ancestors began to look with fear—and reverence—at our fellow planetary inhabitants in the animal kingdom. With little doubt, the man of some millennia before our time had recognized the sting of the cat's claw, or admired the grace, if not the magic, of the falcon as it lifted its wings against the air, and did what no other, save the blowing breeze, could do. With both respect and admiration for such feats among our world's various fauna, our ancient ancestors no doubt also began to contemplate how they might seek to mimic the conveniences of the world around them, and discover ways to turn the forces of the elements in mankind's favor.

That process, along with the conventions of modern science, has continued ever since, and is very much still underway even today. Our agile aircraft mimic the flight of the bird, while our arsenal of weaponry, though it began with fear of tooth and bone, can now outdo the finest armaments that nature could provide. Mankind has utilized the mastery of matter and its manipulation to bend the forces of the natural world to its own desires, and thus instituted a kind of magic that even nature would envy.

But as this continuation of dominance plays out, one can only guess where it could take us next, as there are yet still aspects of nature that have managed to evade us. Creatures that range from the scurrying lizards of the jungle, to the strange and nearly amorphous cephalopods of coral reefs and crannies, are able to blend with their surroundings and literally change the tone and color of their outer surface in order to provide instant camouflage. While man has developed technologies that allow for sight in the darkness, what would it take for humans to match the wolf's ability to peer into darkness with an eye unencumbered by heavy goggles or headgear? And while the unmoving tree can be easily felled by the sharp blade of an axe, the many which remain are able to outlive man by decades, if not centuries... how might a human ever extend his or her longevity to match that of the great oaks of the western American forests? Or, could a human increase their lifespan indefinitely?

All these questions that have challenged us for so long remain at the forefront of scientific pursuit and study. However, many in the modern day feel that we have begun to draw near to the realization of such technologies; furthermore, the rate of growth of existing technologies also seems to be increasing even greater than in the exponential sense. Computer science continues to push further and further into the realm of not just super and exascale computation, but toward realms where the ability to filter consciousness using artificial mechanisms of intelligence may very soon leap from the page of our far-out science fiction, and become the new reality of today.

The concept of *Trans-humanism* is inherent to all this, and while it is no new formulation of expectations regarding where humankind may eventually go, many would argue that current scientific innovations are bringing humans closer to its realization than ever before. To define trans-humanism is no simple task, as it is both a hopeful longing for some, as well as a vile promise of control, paired with the utter relinquishment of our biological capacities for others. The level of controversy it entails has drawn much attention to what have largely become a cultural movement and one that, at times, even bears the hallmarks of an emergent religious denomination. Still others consider trans-humanism the summation of the intellectual movement in America and other parts of the world today, with leading scientists, venture capitalists, and forward-thinkers seeking to expound on where the science of tomorrow will take us. Arguably, the end result will be a humanity that is more heavily influenced by the technology it creates than at any point in history… and perhaps to such a degree that the end result, rather than being human at all, would be most effectively defined as *post-human.*

It is indeed obvious that humanity today faces the ever-encroaching limitations of scarcity; the creation of more bodies is both indicative of our success as a dominant species on Earth, as well as a promise of eventual hardships, when the inevitable troubles of balancing the number of mouths which desire to be fed alongside the food and supplies that remain available will become acutely apparent. Thus, as humankind moves forward, the concept of eventual change—and perhaps even by taking evolution itself into our own hands—becomes almost a necessity for visions of future growth and sustenance.

But should humankind manage to exceed the limitations of our biology, many would rightly argue that, at such a time, the intelligent beings that would result are effectively no longer human at all. Where, then, do the concepts of soul and spirit go? How do we continue to define such things as consciousness, when the potential for a machine to harness it becomes a reality? One might also point out that, in order to be able to formulate the essence of consciousness in another essentially manlike form, a more complete understanding of consciousness would first be required. Much the same, as we seek to understand the elements of existent reality in our midst, humankind may wonder what the intelligent life of tomorrow could actually end up being like… but what if we were to venture to guess that it were already here?

One idea that remains intriguing when paired contextually with Ufology, and yet which remains largely disassociated from the idea of advanced, unidentified aircraft, involves an idea that is concomitant with the study of trans-humanism; it involves the concept of a coming technological "Singularity." Defined roughly, this entails a point where humankind essentially merges with technological systems we design, which eventually leads to the creation of varieties of super-human intelligence.

Singularity has become a hot topic these days. The general concept has been around for the better part of the last century, thanks to the ideas of writers going as far back as Pierre Teilhard de Chardin, and more recently science fiction author Vernor Vinge. However, these days it is most often associated with inventor and trans-humanist advocate Ray Kurzweil. Having emerged as the modern godfather of the Singularity movement (which many liken to being near-religious in several of its facets), Kurzweil's book "*The Singularity is Near*" represents, without question, the most thorough and comprehensive analysis of the subject to-date.

Interestingly, when we look further back at the roots of Singularity, we find references to remarkably similar concepts that appear in the work of computer scientist and UFO researcher Jacques Vallee. A 1975 essay, co-authored with Vallee's associate Francois Meyer, appeared in the journal *Technological Forecasting and Social Change* in the year mentioned under the title "The Dynamics of Long-Term Growth". Here, the ideas expressed were very similar concepts to notions of Singularity expressed by Kurzweil and others today, so far as the long-term growth of human technological systems was greater-than exponential. Though the term "Singularity" was never used specifically, Vallee, like Kurzweil, predicted that sometime in the first half of the twenty first century, we would see the rate of growth of technology begin to expand so quickly that a sort of "singular point" would be reached; Vallee feared this could have grim consequences, when paired alongside steady increases in population growth over time. Specifically, Vallee and Meyer estimated that the target year for this transitional singularity would occur in 2026, whereas in his *The Singularity is Near*, Kurzweil casts his forecast for what he calls "the knew of the curve" at only three years later.

As noted previously, unlike the more optimistic attitudes toward Singularity expressed by Kurzweil and many in the trans-humanist camp today, Vallee and Meyer's paper is more concerned and skeptical, stating that, "the forecast of infinite growth in a finite time interval is absurd. All we can expect of these developments is that some damping effect will take place very soon. The only question is whether this will be accomplished through 'soft regulation' or catastrophe." One could speculate as to what the authors could have meant by the use of such terms as "soft regulation" paired with "catastrophe." Are we to envision Orwellian micro-management of a populace, or perhaps long-term geo-economic collapse that would stem from issues surrounding overpopulation, combined with the poor management of our banking systems? Catastrophe might also represent such things as the harmful after-effects of an EMP weapon, or even coronal mass ejection by the Sun (the likes of which agencies like NASA and NOAA have warned might occur by around 2013). Vallee and Meyer's final statement is perhaps the most cryptic: "It is clear that the rate of growth must eventually decrease. A discussion of the mechanism through which this decrease will take place is beyond the scope of the present study." Vernor Vinge, largely credited with coining the modern use of the term "Singularity," was less nebulous when he wrote for *Omni* back in January 1983 that, "To write a (science fiction) story set more than a century hence, one needs a nuclear war in between ... so that the world remains intelligible."

With all this discussion of dangerous and earth-quaking possibilities that could await us in the future, it is interesting that many have seemed to look to UFOs as a proverbial agent of grace, sent to Earth from lands afar to save us from ourselves. Robert Hastings, author of the book *UFOs and Nukes*, has noted in interviews that, while these craft indeed seem to be not only more highly-advanced than what humans are capable of producing, they are also capable of disarming our weapons systems; thus, this might be a good thing in terms of preventing wide scale destruction as a result of nuclear proliferation. Indeed, this may be the case, but we also must recognize the alternative potential here, too: what *else* could a technology capable of disarming our weapons systems do to us, besides rendering us virtually defenseless from an oncoming attack? Perhaps the notion of the "UFO savior" isn't all it's made out to be.

Clearly, when it comes to UFOs, we are dealing with some variety of technology that exceeds those sciences known to us today. To compare this again with Singularity, we see that The Singularity Institute has defined the term as literally representing, "the technological creation of smarter-than-human intelligence." With UFOs, perhaps we are already dealing with some technological manifestation that exceeds natural human intelligence.

Let us think for a moment now, and examine the apparent lack of progress that has taken place over the decades in terms of understanding more completely what the UFO enigma seems to be offering us. To proceed further from where we stand at present, it appears that we may indeed have to revise our methodology, which up to now has largely consisted of studying past UFO reports, and trying to extract details, documents, and government files pertaining to these past occurrences. Should we instead cast our gaze in the other direction, and begin to consider whether there might be emergent technologies—perhaps even futuristic sciences in development today—that will help to bridge the proverbial gap between where we stand now, and those awe-inspiring aircraft we've pursued since the days when the literal dust of the Second World War had yet to settle? Regardless, if Kurzweil and others are right in their expectations for how science of the coming years will change humanity as we know it, there may be little that could be done in terms of preventing technological leaps that will, if anything, place us directly before the enigma known today as

Ufology… and perhaps within reach of an apparent technology that far exceeds us.

BIO: Micah Hanks is author of several books, including *Magic, Mysticism and the Molecule*, *Reynolds Mansion: An Invitation to the Past,* and his 2012 New Page Books release, *The UFO Singularity and his newest book, The Ghost Rockets.* Hanks is also an executive editor for *Intrepid Magazine*, and consulting editor for *FATE Magazine* and *The Journal of Anomalous Sciences.* He also writes for a variety of other publications including *UFO Magazine, Mysterious Universe*, and *New Dawn.* Hanks has appeared on numerous TV and radio programs, including National Geographic's *Paranatural*, the History Channel's *Guts and Bolts*, *CNN Radio*, and *The Jeff Rense Program.* He also produces a weekly podcast that follows his research at his popular website, www.gralienreport.com.

Ventre Note: In 2016, Google's program *AlphaGo*, learned to play the Go game by playing against itself. It somehow learned to calculate insightful moves and out-maneuver the best human players. Its programmers don't know how the program calculated its moves. I'm waiting for when AI can accurately pick stocks……

Adam's sin caused the curse of aging and death in Genesis 3. Is Transhumanism a repeat of Genesis 5 when Satan told Eve that she can be like God? Do we really want to improve on nature or the image of our creator and engineer a better human? Should we go beyond wellness to enhancements? Should we design babies? Is our issue health or an envious sinful heart and soul? Does genetically altering man disqualify him from entrance into heaven? "BIOPS", the British Institute of Post-human Studies writes:

"The fact is we remain shackled by our primitive Darwinian brains. Humanity for whatever progress we have made, is the result of an unguided, natural, 3.8 billion-year-long experiment of chemistry....[we must] fundamentally revolutionize what it means to be human by way of technological advancements." The transhumanist FAQ, created and compiled by transhumanists and whose goal is to "provide a reliable source of information about transhumanism" provides insight into their idea of "religion": "Some of the prospects that used to be the exclusive thunder of the religious institutions, such as very long lifespan, unfading bliss, and godlike intelligence, are being discussed by transhumanists as hypothetical future engineering achievements."

"The arguments for various transhumanist technologies often confuse the notion of morality. Genetic engineering, a key component in transhumanist thought, is "one of the most moral things we can do," says Max More, self-proclaimed founder of the modern transhumanist movement. *I can and so I should because I want to; my body, my choice. It's all about me and my wants.* These are the attitudes often presented. If we can mix the genes of animals with the genes of human beings, perhaps with the initial charitable motivation to create organs for transplants, then as the transhumanists propose, we can also be designing custom human-animal hybrids: humans with wings to fly or humans with centaur-like legs, the imagination reels at the permutations, but far from utopic, this free-for-all menagerie demonstrates a failure to appreciate what it means to be human. And it can only get worse if technologically "enhanced" humans see themselves as superior to non-technologically altered human beings; Auschwitz all over again?"

"The problem with Transhumanism is the attitude of the Transhumanists and their rejection of God. There is no limit to dehumanization in our desire to engineer the perfect human."

(Courtesy *Aleteia* by Dr. Eugene Gan April 2015)

Chapter Five

Revelation

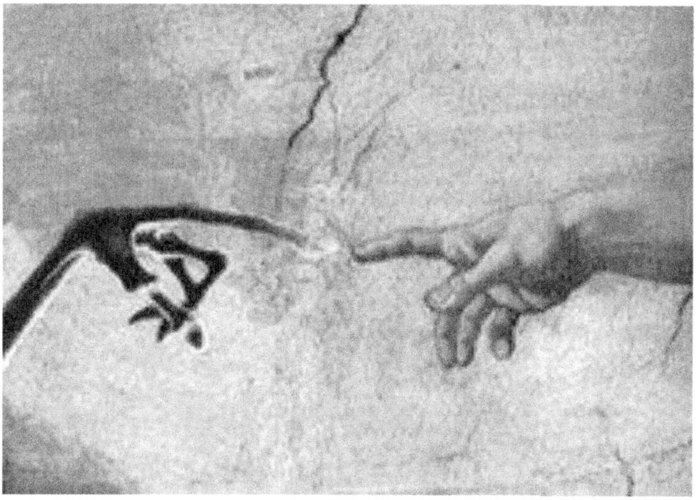

"There is a skeleton in every closet"

I obviously wrote the first chapter as a parable and I never did pick up a hitch hiker but I thought it was a good way to tell one possible explanation for our development. Most authors are so afraid of the religious or scientific community that they would not dare tell this story. We will see if the TV stations also shy aware in fear of losing sponsors. I thought the History Channel might have the courage but they didn't.

I hope you are now questioning everything you've been taught and are asking yourself, "What is the String Theory that explains everything?" The String Theory for how we became us would be in this order:

1. Creation because it is the easiest and most accepted answer for everything. An all-powerful Being answers all questions and doubts. "Welcome to Heaven but please close the door upon entry. Welcome to Hell but he who enters here, give's up all hope."
2. Alien intervention because it fills in the evolutionary missing links and of course they have superior technology like a God but we still need to produce the alien to the public. There is also the question of deception.
3. And lastly, Evolution because it has too many holes.

If we ask, "What is the String Theory for where do "They" and all that is unexplained but interlinked come from?" The answer would be inter-dimensional. There are too many real but unexplained paranormal events from ghosts and black eyed kids to fairies and angels to glimpses of creatures like Bigfoot and Mothman to ETs. What if they are all related to a dimension right around us that some pass through by accident and others pass through by design? Isn't Heaven a dimension? God sent his only son to put an end to the open reign of Satan which took place prior to Jesus' birth. Unlike today's church, about 20% of everything Jesus said was to combat evil and demons.

But more importantly, how can we truly advance as a species until we know how we got here? How can we decide on our purpose until we know what the purpose of us is? If a superior Being created us then we should all be in harmony with nature and non-violence. If we were genetically engineered then we should continue that engineering to reach perfection. If we evolved then we should continue the survival of the fittest pursuit of money and technology with no regard to ethics or morality.

Something has changed on earth. I can't tell you an exact date. You can see an absolute progression in our modern history. Eighty percent of all serial killings have occurred since 1950. In 1952, the CIA formed the Collins Elite to investigate the paranormal. In the mid 1970's, we get the ritualistic cattle mutilations with no media coverage and law enforcement kept on the outside. An October 14, 1976 FBI memo states that, "mutilations of cattle are only the forerunner of mutilations of human beings". Between 1975 and 1979, there were over 10,000 cattle mutilations. Besides surgical removal of organs, the carcasses are found with all blood drained and predators avoid them. Black helicopters are also seen in the area yet the government surely has the resources to fund their own research. The Gomez ranch near Dulce lost over 50 cattle. The cattle were being marked with a potassium-magnesium substance that could be seen with a black light at night. Are the helicopters actually built by ETs with ET pilots or are they a branch of our Military called the Night Stalkers who appease ancient deities in exchange for supernatural weapons? Or do "They" need genetic material to reconstruct themselves on this planet? Cattle DNA are only 80% similar to human DNA. Does this also explain the 4000 people a year in the U.S. that just disappears? Make no mistake, the Jack the Ripper murders were done for the same reason. There was no Jack, Jack!

The alien abduction scenario also changed from creatures in uniform in space ships to late night Greys appearing out of the darkness of the corner of your room to abduct you to an altered state of reality. Since 1990, exorcisms performed have increased from six per year to over 1300 per year.

Who was behind the assassinations of President Kennedy and Pope John Paul I? Why do honest leaders get killed? Why does the U.S. government have FEMA internment camps and want everyone tracked with RFID chips and all guns confiscated? Why has U.S. foreign policy gone from benevolent to imperialistic? Why are jobs moved from the U.S. to ruthless China who is a military enemy of the U.S.? Nothing regarding the September 11 World Trade Center attack makes sense. There is a plot in this nation and around the world to wrestle control of government away from the people so they can be enslaved and controlled and genetically altered against their will. Dissenters are silenced not praised. Where do the thousands of missing persons really go? All throughout history, children and young adults have been taken by so called "fairies and boogeymen" who were actually the Fallen in disguise. Are alien abductions and hybrid humans really alien? What if these hybrids are a modern day Nephilim being engineered or created by the Fallen to prevent the return of Christ by altering us genetically from the image of our creator no different than the vampires or zombies in vogue on TV and in movies?

A close look at our media and education systems, which understand that 70% of people will believe whatever an authority figure says, proves that every effort is being made to pull us away from Christianity and moral values and substitute a liberal anything goes disinformation agenda. The U.S. is being deconstructed from within where nationalism is a four letter word and our economy builds up our enemies. It makes no sense and it makes perfect sense if the Fallen have infiltrated government and corporations.

In a recent poll in Great Britain, only 33% believed in God and less than half were affiliated with a religion. The numbers are more atheistic with the young. The Catholic Church has tried to be politically correct and appeal to the masses by getting away from scaring people about evil and the devil but attendees continue to drop and nearly a third of all priests and pastors do not believe Satan is a real entity. I say "WTF happened in one lifetime?"

We continue to put our faith in atheistic science that has only cured two diseases or plagues; polio and small pox yet we all believe they have the answer or a pill for everything. Science cannot or will not explain the unexplained because we will then have no need for science. What you bind on earth will be bound in heaven. Understand the preternatural but don't worship it. Become a student of the supernatural which are miracles from God. What if preternatural influence is and always has been the greatest influence on our events? Is this thinking akin to the dark ages or were they correct about many of their myths and beliefs? Make no mistake; any talk of a New World Order is absolutely just talk regarding the Fallen and their control of humanity. These secret societies are not run by greedy bankers and CEO's and a New World Order is a deception for the Old World Order; the Fallen that have always been here!

I wrote three books since I retired from UPS. This is my fifth and my next book, *Case for UFOs* will be my last book that I intend to write. I have other goals on my bucket list. I intend to run for County Commissioner and then Congress.

If this book is found by some post-apocalyptic society or by arriving space travelers, it could easily be mistaken for our historical record and then the scientists would create their "*Theory of Genetic Engineering of the Human Race*". They would jealously stick to that theory and debunk all others. You see how easy it is. . . . . . It's hard to find answers in a field where there aren't any. . . . .

"The suppression of uncomfortable ideas may be common in religion and politics, but it is not the path to knowledge, it has no place in science." -- Carl Sagan 1980

(I purchased this 1992 painting from Charles Lang in Salem Mass. The kids absolutely look like mine in hair color and age.)

I love this picture!

"The Truth can only be glimpsed through the eyes of death." – *Inferno*

"In war, fathers bury their sons. In peace, sons bury their fathers"- *The Immortals*

A LETTER TO MY GREAT GRAND CHILDREN:

Hopefully you know of me. God bless you because God put you here. As long as you have grandparents, parents, children and pets, you'll be loved. The world you inhabit is vastly different than the one I grew up in. You have better technology and medicine. The one I grew up in was a white male dominated America that got things done and was the world's super power and believed in God. I hope China is not in charge in your time. China is a communist dictatorship where people have very few rights. America is gambling that we can build up China and increase trade yet China increases its military while we have fallen into debt and our people want socialism which kills motivation. Politicians need votes so they give the people what they want; not what they need. Your parents and grandparents grew up under the threat of terrorism.

Their parents grew up under the threat of nuclear war. I hope you have better leaders and are not living under the threat of bio-engineered and nano-technology threats.

My America was white male dominated who were hard on everyone including themselves but we had low crime and an exaggerated media fake news belief that racism was rampant. Affirmative Action was a quota system where the ends justified the means and discriminated against Asian and white males in violation of the 14th Amendment. Instead, what was needed was the elimination of race and gender questions from all applications. Everything this modern world is was created by Europeans and Americans. As I write this, whites seem to be on the decline population wise due to their own birth self-control and common sense and your world will be well on the path of multiculturalism and diversity. I was a third generation immigrant and my two children, Nolan and Vanessa, were the first Ventre's to earn a college degree. I attended excellent public schools on Long Island and my children did the same in Northern New Jersey which now seem to be in decline again due to quotas and a lack of discipline. My generation and my parent's generation had pride in America yet it now seems to be under attack by left wing liberal groups and minorities. My country is being brought down to the level of rap music. The school system and media seem to rewrite history or ignore the truth only to attack America which is the freest and kindest country on the planet. We rebuilt Germany and Japan after

WWII; no other country had ever been so generous. We contribute more per person to charities than any other country. We are portrayed as greedy hostile racists by the media and academia. The media sells out for viewership and Politicians for votes. They are the two ends of the same stick and both are corrupt. I believe a patriotic President will arise. Do the research and find out the truth for yourself. Believe your lying eyes. America has been good to the five generations that got you here; stand up for America, freedom and your Constitution! I am a self-made millionaire who started working at eleven and is at peace with himself and with what I have accomplished; mainly on my own. I have never received any government assistance and I hope you never do either.

My father's side of the family was butchers. My mother's side of the family was steel workers. Always work hard and never lie, cheat or steal. Compete; be a little better than the next person but don't brag. Everything you do comes back at you. Trust no one but family. Most people are like floor wax; shiny on the outside but lacking depth. People vote for who they like and then require no more from them than themselves. Stay away from gambling, drugs and alcohol. Respect the Ten Commandments and the Bill of Rights. The Kingdom of God is within you. When you do things for the right reasons, you are in the Kingdom of God. Respect the police, military and adults. Love your parents and children. Protect your inheritance even though nothing given to you is worth as much as something earned and work to live; don't live to work. And I hope I was able to see you get born. (10)

LOVE,
Your Great Grand Father
John J. Ventre

In John Milton's 1667 epic poem *Paradise Lost*, he said that angels and demons can shape shift. They can also build in an hour what it would take many men a lifetime to build. The half human-half demon Nephilim built the *Tower of Babel*, *King Solomon's Temple* and the great *Pyramids*. The half human-half creature Egyptian gods of Horus, Toth, Anubis and Ra were actually fallen angels. Milton went blind and dictated much of this work.

When the end comes, ***"Do not go gentle into that good night"***

Do not go gentle into that good night,
Old age should burn and rave at close of day;
Rage, rage against the dying of the light.

Though wise men at their end know dark is right,
Because their words had forked no lightning they
Do not go gentle into that good night.

Good men, the last wave by, crying how bright
Their frail deeds might have danced in a green bay,
Rage, rage against the dying of the light.

Wild men who caught and sang the sun in flight,
And learn, too late, they grieved it on its way,
Do not go gentle into that good night.

Grave men, near death, who see with blinding sight
Blind eyes could blaze like meteors and be gay,
Rage, rage against the dying of the light.

And you, my father, there on the sad height,
Curse, bless, me now with your fierce tears, I pray.
Do not go gentle into that good night.
Rage, rage against the dying of the light.

Courtesy Dylan Thomas, 1914 – 1953

Case for UFOs
MAKE UFOLOGY GREAT AGAIN
John J Ventre's
Official YouTube Channel
www.johnventre.blogspot.co.uk

2015
amazon.com
e-Books available
2016
Case for UFOs
John J. Ventre
THE UFOLOGIST
John J.Ventre
An Alternative History of Mankind
John J.Ventre
UFOs over PENNSYLVANIA
John J. Ventre
John J. Ventre
APOPHIS 2029
The Coming Mass Extinction ...
2015
2015
2013

Chapter Six

Origin of the Phenomena

How can we truly advance as a species until we know how we got here? How can we decide on our purpose until we know what the purpose of us is? If a superior Being created us, then we should all be in harmony with nature and non-violence and human equality guided by morality. If we were genetically engineered then we should continue that engineering by enhancing our DNA to reach our pinnacle of perfection. I don't think I want to be a new species. We would no longer be in the image of our creator and wouldn't this in essence avert Satan's destruction? If we evolved with no God then we should continue the Darwinian survival of the fittest pursuit of money and technology and be the best sinners possible since we are just animals and the end justifies the means. We should protect our planets resources from overpopulation by eugenically eliminating the weaker strains of humans from the genetic pool. Hasn't evolution taught us to not believe in God but to put our faith in the infallibility of science and the coming ETs? This duplicity is our single most important question.

Here are some possible explanations for the UFO phenomena. Are we dealing with super technology or the preternatural?

Extraterrestrial hypothesis (**ETH**), proposed by Major Keyhoe after the Thomas Mantell incident, theorizes that aliens travel here from other planets. Keyhoe shifted the burden of proof to the government. But the distances are vast and UFOs have never been seen approaching from deep space even though statistically there should be life in space. The theory of evolution makes the chances of a genetic match zero. There are over 1000 sightings per month. Wouldn't that indicate a massive fleet is here? There are radar, photo and government documents. In 1963, Carl Sagan theorized that we would be visited every 10,000 years by a new species. Why are SETI and NASA silent? Are they placebos?

Ancient Astronaut Theory (**AA**), we've misidentified angels and God and the bible. ET's have been here from our beginning and genetically upgraded us from hominids and actively participate in our history. Ancient structures, rock carvings and cave paintings along with the Hindu Mahabharata seem to support this. Ancient Alien Theory is blasphemy and falls under **ETH.**

Prison-**Z**oo Earth- Aliens look like us and originally used earth like a Devils Island or Botany Bay for the unwanted or we are being contained here for our own good. Zoo earth maintains that species are dropped off and negate earth evolution. Prison-Zoo earth falls under **ETH**.

Interdimensional or **U**ltraterrestrial hypotheses **(UTH)** theorizes there are eleven dimensions and that they exist on a different plane or parallel universe but are indigenous to earth and have always co-existed with us. Our Quantum physics attempts to explain them. They may create the perception of a UFO by manipulating matter or energy. Jesus said, "*My Kingdom is not of this world*"- John 18:36.

Demonic- ETs are shape shifting Fallen Angels and exist in a malevolent dimension and can enter ours and are deliberately disguised as ET. The fact that they hide, operate at night and avoid open contact may support this. Fallen Angels can materialize craft or telepathically project them and this is what we are experiencing. God gave Lucifer two thirds of the universe and he is the prince of the air (UFOs) and was an angel of light (orbs). Their goal is to draw us away from belief in Christ, corrupt our DNA and ultimately deceive us. This is the Great Deception at the Tribulation. We will be told the Christians were taken by aliens, not God. They have also mated with us in the past and produced the Nephilim. Altered state CE-4 and demonic possession are one in the same. Demonic falls under **UTH**.

Cryptoterrestrial **(CTH)** or hollow earth proposed by Mac Tonnies- They co-exists with us on this planet either in inner earth or under the oceans. Biologically could this explain abductions for a DNA match by advanced Atlanteans, evolved reptiles or dinosaurs? But again, how do you explain the Grey unisex look and unworkable large head to slim hip proportions for a natural birth, if they are birthed?

Extratemporal time travel from the future where they are us returning for a look or in need of something or to fix an event. This is a biological way an exchange of DNA could work during abductions and would explain their ability to prophesize future events (nuclear war, environment, Fatima). But how do you explain the Grey unisex look and unworkable large head to slim hip proportions for a natural birth, if they are birthed? Is the Grey a worker or android?

Hoax- Which makes up about 10% of cases.

Natural phenomena hypothesis- science can explain everything, of course.

Psychological- Carl Jung believed that some UFOs are a projection of our mind in response to our beliefs but that some UFOs show signs of intelligent guidance by quasi human pilots. Others say magnetic fields or drugs can cause UFO hallucinations. There is a mass delusion or collective schizophrenia where we have replaced séances and mediums with UFOs. J Allen Hynek believed we might be projecting these sightings with our mind and telekinesis.

Military- the Air Force or Navy uses UFOs as a cover story for our own advanced military craft. A UFO was back engineered from recovered Nazi technology (1936 Black Forest crash) through Project Paperclip and some of the subsequent crashes were our test flights (Roswell). We test our new weapons in foreign countries like the 1977 Colares Brazil case. The 1984 Hudson Valley sightings and 1997 Phoenix lights sightings were of our craft which make up *Project Solar Warden*. The military is involved in cattle mutilations and abductions (***MILabs***) and abductees are brought to underground bases. Disinformation and staged events like the Richard Doty hoax of Linda Moulton Howe for example along with MK-Ultra, Collins Elite and Operation Often. The CIA debunking of UFOs was deliberate to keep scientists and the media from investigating. The Collins Elite concluded there were no UFOs, just paranormal activity by demons.

Programmers- The pending release of PC game *No Man's Sky*- in which a supercomputer generated trillions of inhabited worlds after being given the guidelines for its universe by human programmers- raises questions as to whether a more advanced civilization could create our reality with exponentially more powerful computers. Over the past 5 years, mainstream physicists have begun to explore whether our "universe" could be a hologram, and prominent figures like *Space X* CEO Elon Musk have been fascinated with the possibility. In this theory, the "Big Bang" was basically the program itself initiating or turning on, and it has been evolving with the guidelines given to it ever since. This would be not unlike *The Matrix* movies starring Keanu Reeves, in which an alternate reality is "projected" for us. This could explain why UFOs seemingly pop in and out of our reality and exhibit flight characteristics not consistent with known physics: it's the programmers checking in on the simulation at various places and times, much like a child lifting the lid off of an ant colony. It could also explain why so many given access to the "truth" of UFOs and extraterrestrials refuse to talk about it: beyond any security clearances or oaths, the reality that we do not actually exist- but are simply a manifestation of an artificial program- is too upsetting to share, because it would invalidate our entire existence. (Courtesy James Krug).

None or a **C**ombination of all of the above?

How would you rank these when the only source of data comes from the UFO and what they want us to see? Each theory has its own extensive convincing kaleidoscope history but none have enough empirical evidence. They all can't be correct. My guess is, like the cases we investigate; only around 10% are real while 90% are deliberate C.I.A. or entity disinformation or misdirection. But which 10% is real? Are inter-dimensional and demonic the same?

In April of 2017, nineteen of my Pa MUFON Investigators discussed these possibilities and voted on each category. Two investigators abstained due to lack of evidence. ETH received the most first place votes, Ancient Alien the most second place votes and Military the most third place votes. There were 98 total points and Ancient Alien received 26, ETH 25, Military 15, UTH 13, Combo 11, Demonic 4, Prison 2, Psychological and Programmers 1 each; Hoax, CTH, Extratemporal and Natural zero votes. My question is, how well read are the investigators on all possibilities? Were they influenced by the Ancient Alien TV series and movies that stress ETs are from space? Wouldn't the disinformation choice be the most popular and the true source be hidden? Read my book, "*The Ufologist*" for a perspective on the demonic and UFOs.

Scientist Dr. Carl Sagan in his book, *"Intelligent Life in the Universe"* indicated Earth had likely been visited by extraterrestrials. He states: *"Sumer was an early–perhaps the first - civilization the contemporary sense on the planet Earth. It was founded in the fourth millennium B.C. or earlier. We don't know where the Sumerians came from. I feel that if the Sumerian civilization is depicted by the descendants of the Sumerians themselves to be of non-human origin, the relevant legends should be examined carefully."* (Page 456) He goes on to ask, *"What might an advanced extraterrestrial civilization want from us?"*......He answered his own question by stating, *"One of the primary motivations for the exploration of the New World was to convert the inhabitants to Christianity — peacefully if possible — forcefully if necessary. Can we exclude the possibility of an extraterrestrial evangelism? "*(Page 463)

rious Melville Mops are (l.—r.) Front — Ed Hodnett, Tom Spitz, Tim
ewski. Rear — Gene McManus, Bob Bern, Joe Dudas, John
ario, Rosey Disponzio, Gene Hagner, John Ventry, Tom Fuchs.

At UPS softball game in 1981. They spelled my name wrong…..

Chapter Seven

About the Author

John Ventre is an author, lecturer, and TV show co-host and an occasional security consultant for the Gerson Lehrman Group. He is the retired Pennsylvania State Security and Public Affairs Director for UPS and was his company's liaison to his local Congressman and was elected to the Republican Committee. John used to also head up his company's crisis management team for three states.

John was the Pa State Director for the Mutual UFO Network and was MUFONs first multi-state director managing seven states in the north east for ten years. John is the author of the novels: *12/21/2012 A Prophecy*, *The Day After 2012*, *UFOs over Pennsylvania*, *Apophis 2029* and *An Alternative History of Mankind.* It was John's research into end time prophecy and ancient cultures that got him interested in UFOs in 1996. Many cultures spoke of star people or people from the sky which gave them advanced knowledge which interested John in UFOs. The more John researched, the more he found. John was a comicon; *Famous Monsters of Filmland*; *Fate* magazine reader in his younger days. John didn't choose Ufology; it chose him.

John was a member of the FBI's Infra-Gard group and the DHS Regional Business Coalition. John is also a lifetime member of the NRA. John has served on the Board of Directors for Juvenile Diabetes, the Westmoreland Economic Growth Connection and Rotary. John is a United Way Tocqueville Society member for charitable giving and is his Rotary Club President. John is the co-inventor of the *Thor Wood Splitter* and owns the UFO themed Mexican restaurant trademark *Flying Salsa.*

John appeared in the Discovery Channels *UFOs over Earth* series in 2008 and the History Channels *UFO Hunters* in 2009, the *Anderson Cooper show* in 2012, Destination America's *Alien Mysteries* and History's *Ancient Aliens* (cameo) in 2013 and H2's (History) *Hangar 1: The UFO Files* and PCTV21's *UFOs over Pittsburgh* in 2014 through the present which changed its name to *The String Theory of the Unexplained* in 2017 and *Close Encounters* for Discovery Science in 2015. John has appeared on numerous radio shows and is a speaker at various UFO and paranormal conferences such as the MUFON and Paradigm Symposium's, UFO Congress and Fortean Conference's. John has also lectured at Duquesne and Drexel Universities on UFOs along with the Wizard World Comicon in 2015. John gives thirteen different lecture presentations: *End Time Prophecy, The Case for*

UFOs, UFOs in Art and History, The Chronology of UFOs, Anderson Cooper and the Case for UFOs, UFOs and the Media, An Alternative History, My Haunted Story, String Theory of the Unexplained, Eerie Pa, Native American Superstitions, Do you know the Paranormal and the 2008 Pa UFO Wave.

John has come full circle with his research into alternative sciences and theories which have strongly led him back to Jesus since 2014 when he had an angel-demon encounter (see *The Ufologist* book). John now believes that God did create the universe fully aged and seeded earth with life. God observes his creation and there is no evolution. God created Adam to combat Lucifer who rebelled against Jesus, who in the spirit observed the fall of Lucifer from Heaven. The Bible only describes the family line of Adam and may allow for other creatures and evolution. Jesus was the second Adam and defeated Satan for our salvation if you want it. We and the angels were always given free will. So choose! My theories cannot be found in scripture of which I am poorly versed.

Fight me if you wish but I'm old for a reason!

Buy American = Save the Economy

If we are to benefit from this splendid myth we have created, we must never lose sight of the fact that it is – only a myth . . . Hilary Evans.

Chapter Eight

References and Suggested Reading

1. ***Above Top Secret by Timothy Good***
2. ***Alien Viruses by Dr Robert Wood.***
3. ***Apophis 2029 by John Ventre.***
4. ***The Economist, since 1843.***
5. ***Our Haunted Planet by John Keel.***
6. ***The Report on UFOs by Edward J. Ruppelt.***
7. ***UFOs and the National Security State by Richard Dolan.***
8. ***UFOs in Wartime by Mack Maloney.***
9. ***UFOs over Pennsylvania by John Ventre.***
10. ***Paraphrased from a Newsmax article by Ben Stiller.***
11. ***Wonders in the Sky by Jacques Vallee.***

A "3D"image of the Shroud of Turin was created in 2018 showing the true face of Jesus. He stood 5' 11"with long arms and legs. Free Masons contend that Jesus was 5' 6" and hunchbacked with a large nose which only proves their disdain for Christianity:

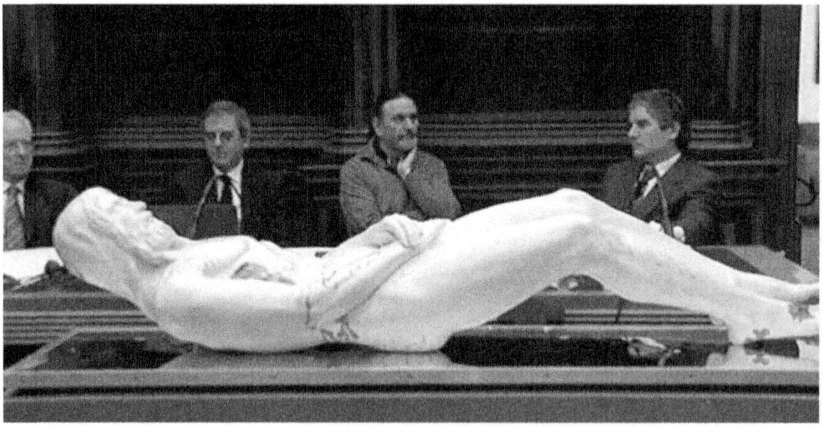

Philly MUFON Conference September 2010.

Pittsburgh MUFON Conference October 2011.

Son Nolan, Veronica, daughter Vanessa, Seth 2013

Roswell Museum July 2013.

Filming of "*Hangar 1*" TV series September 2013.

"If "They" discover you first, then there is an old rule of thumb that "They" are your technological superiors."

Philly MUFON Conference October 2013.

2014 Filming Close Encounters in Toronto

I've adopted five Doberman's from shelters. Man's best friend and more loyal than any spouse could be. My next Dobie will be named Majestic since my dogs live around 12 years:

Good Doggy	**1994-2004**
Precious	**1990-1999**
Mama Bear	**1999-2011**
Poppa Bear	**2000-2012**
Apophis	**2011-present**

May 10, 2014

April 11, 2015

Atomic Testing Museum July 2017

Hangar 1 cast

Did you know Pamela Anderson was supposed to play Scully and not Gillian Anderson?

When I was growing up, I loved boxing. Iceland is the only free country that bans boxing. I'm now a big MMA fan and took three years of kickboxing until I injured my Achilles tendon. I think boxing should limit its fights to 25 minutes max or eight rounds in order to protect the boxers from concussion. MMA champion fights are five- five minute rounds and non-championship fights are three- five minute rounds. Boxing gloves are meant to protect the knuckles, not the head. You can play baseball but you can't play fighting. . . .

My Child...

You may not know me, but I know everything about you. Psalm 139:1 I know when you sit down and when you rise up. Psalm 139:2 I am familiar with all your ways. Psalm 139:3 Even the very hairs on your head are numbered. Matthew 10:29-31 For you were made in my image. Genesis 1:27 In me you live and move and have your being. Acts 17:28 For you are my offspring. Acts 17:28 I knew you even before you were conceived. Jeremiah 1:4-5 I chose you when I planned creation. Ephesians 1:11-12 You were not a mistake, for all your days are written in my book. Psalm 139:15-16 I determined the exact time of your birth and where you would live. Acts 17:26 You are fearfully and wonderfully made. Psalm 139:14 I knit you together in your mother's womb. Psalm 139:13 And brought you forth on the day you were born. Psalm 71:6 I have been misrepresented by those who don't know me. John 8:41-44 I am not distant and angry, but am the complete expression of love. 1 John 4:16 And it is my desire to lavish my love on you. 1 John 3:1 Simply because you are my child and I am your Father. 1 John 3:1 I offer you more than your earthly father ever could. Matthew 7:11 For I am the perfect Father. Matthew 5:48 Every good gift that you receive comes from my hand. James 1:17 For I am your provider and I meet all your needs. Matthew 6:31-33 My plan for your future has always been filled with hope. Jeremiah 29:11 Because I love you with an everlasting love. Jeremiah 31:3 My thoughts toward you are countless as the sand on the seashore. Psalms 139:17-18 And I rejoice over you with singing. Zephaniah 3:17 I will never stop doing good to you. Jeremiah 32:40 For you are my treasured possession. Exodus 19:5 I desire to establish you with all my heart and all my soul. Jeremiah 32:41 And I want to show you great and marvelous things. Jeremiah 33:3 If you seek me with all your heart, you will find me. Deuteronomy 4:29 Delight in me and I will give you the desires of your heart. Psalm 37:4 For it is I who gave you those desires. Philippians 2:13 I am able to do more for you than you could possibly imagine. Ephesians 3:20 For I am your greatest encourager. 2 Thessalonians 2:16-17 I am also the Father who comforts you in all your troubles. 2 Corinthians 1:3-4 When you are brokenhearted, I am close to you. Psalm 34:18 As a shepherd carries a lamb, I have carried you close to my heart. Isaiah 40:11 One day I will wipe away every tear from your eyes. Revelation 21:3-4 And I'll take away all the pain you have suffered on this earth. Revelation 21:3-4 I am your Father, and I love you even as I love my son, Jesus. John 17:23 For in Jesus, my love for you is revealed. John 17:26 He is the exact representation of my being. Hebrews 1:3 He came to demonstrate that I am for you, not against you. Romans 8:31 And to tell you that I am not counting your sins. 2 Corinthians 5:18-19 Jesus died so that you and I could be reconciled. 2 Corinthians 5:18-19 His death was the ultimate expression of my love for you. 1 John 4:10 I gave up everything I loved that I might gain your love. Romans 8:31-32 If you receive the gift of my son, Jesus, you receive me. 1 John 2:23 And nothing will ever separate you from my love again. Romans 8:38-39 Come home and I'll throw the biggest party heaven has ever seen. Luke 15:7 I have always been Father and will always be Father. Ephesians 3:14-15 My question is…will you be my child? John 1:12-13 I am waiting for you. Luke 15:11-32

Love, Your Dad

Almighty God

What do you see?

I lectured at David Paulides 2018 event in Colorado

Make America Great Again!

At local rally for law enforcement, wearing my vest. . . .

I ran into another retired UPS Exec while working the polls; Kelly Washington. I was elected to the Republican Committee.

I decided to run for Westmoreland County Commissioner in May 2019. Someone interfered with my election when thousands of my robo-calls went off from 10 pm to 2 am. I came in third…..

Printed in Great Britain
by Amazon

31957306R00126